EASY
CARD
TRICKS

hamlyn

EASY
CARD
TRICKS

Peter Arnold

An Hachette UK Company
www.hachette.co.uk

First published in Great Britain in 2002 by
Hamlyn, a division of Octopus Publishing Group Ltd
Endeavour House
189 Shaftesbury Avenue
London
WC2H 8JY
www.octopusbooksusa.com

This edition published in 2013

Distributed in the US by
Hachette Book Group USA
237 Park Avenue
New York NY 10017 USA

Distributed in Canada by
Canadian Manda Group
165 Dufferin Street
Toronto, Ontario, Canada M6K 3H6

ISBN: 978-0-600-62504-9

A CIP catalogue record for this book is available from the British Library

Page make-up and illustrations by Publish on Demand Ltd.

Card designs based on Waddingtons No. 1 Playing Cards.

WADDINGTONS NO. 1 PLAYING CARDS © 2002 Hasbro Inc.
Used with kind permission.

Printed and bound in China

10 9 8 7 6 5 4 3 2 1

Contents

Introduction

The purpose of this book is to give a reader with no previous knowledge of card tricks enough skills and tricks to entertain and their mystify friends for half-an-hour or so.

The book includes tricks that need no special skills at all, some that need a few pieces of simple equipment, such as a handkerchief or a pen and paper, and others that require conjuring skills such as false shuffles, glides, double lifts and palms, all of which are described.

The main thing to remember, once you have mastered all these skills and tricks, is that what mainly separates one performance or performer from another is presentation. A cold presentation of a trick with the air of 'Look at this, aren't I clever', does not entertain anybody. You need to dress up a trick with a story and if possible a few jokes. You need to be seen to be having fun yourself for your audience to share the pleasure.

In the business, the commentary surrounding a trick is called the 'patter'. Do not be afraid to dress up your performance with seemingly irrelevant asides. This sort of patter helps to keeps your audience interested and it diverts their attention from something you might be doing with the cards which you might not want them to think about too closely. This is called misdirection.

One of the main weapons of the magician, which is not understood by many people in the audience, is the value of subtle, or even blatant misdirection. Sometimes you need to do something with the cards in your hand, such as palming the top card, and you'd like the audience to be looking somewhere else. Simply looking at them and saying something outrageous will have them watching your face while you do the dirty deed at waist level. Sometimes you can turn your back on the audience, pretending it's so that you 'don't see which pile is being chosen' or 'which card is being shown to the audience', while really you are making a subtle adjustment to the cards in your hand.

The patter can also be used to mislead the audience about what you or they have done; for example, which pile was which, or which pile contains which cards. Don't worry about telling blatant lies, such as 'From this shuffled pack, you have chosen...', when the pack was carefully not shuffled at all. If the patter has been entertaining, the audience will not remember that at the beginning you did *not* actually shuffle the pack.

Once you are confident enough to string a few tricks together, build on it. The next step is to personalize the tricks by adding little touches of your own. And of course once you have mastered the various sleights you can invent your own tricks. (Incidentally, many magicians shy from calling their tricks 'tricks' – they prefer such words as 'effects' or 'experiments'.)

Think of packs of cards as your tools and have two or three packs of the same design, so that you can make false cards to blend in with regular packs where necessary (a couple of tricks in this book that involve using a spare card to make a false card). Use cards that have a white border around the pattern on the back. This allows you to mix face-up and face-down cards so that they do not reveal themselves if they are only slightly out of alignment. If you are going to entertain friends with a routine, and you need to slip cards into your pocket or produce a prepared pack, make sure that you are wearing clothes with plenty of deep pockets.

If you are going to perform a trick with a prepared pack (some are included in this book), perform it at the start of your routine, so that you can use the same pack for the subsequent tricks. Otherwise you will need to introduce a new pack during your routine, which will need an explanation. New or nearly new cards are most pleasant to use and most easily manipulated.

Do not repeat tricks, however hard the audience press you. Somebody will spot something and claim they know how you do it. If you are putting on a little show, however informal, perform your best trick last, and do not be persuaded to do any more, as this will only provide an anticlimax.

Above all, practise your tricks before showing them off so that nothing can go wrong – but if it does, and you cannot put it right, smile gracefully and go on to the next one, explaining that even magicians have gremlins. The important thing is to appear professional, and to give the impression that you enjoy what you are doing and that you want the audience to enjoy it, too.

Sleights and shuffles

This chapter explains the sleights of hand, the false shuffles, the double lift and the other tricks of the magicians craft. Once you have mastered these, you can invent new tricks or adapt old ones and can consider yourself a magician.

Normal overhand shuffle

This is the most popular shuffle when playing cards, and one that you should perfect, because it is easily adapted to certain false shuffles.

In this description, if you are left-handed, merely transpose right and left.

1 Hold the pack face down in the fingers of your left hand, with your left thumb holding the pack on the top. With your right hand grasp the majority of the cards from the bottom of the pack, with your right-hand fingers holding the cards at the short side of the pack furthest from you and your right thumb at the side nearest. This is called an undercut.

2 With your left thumb pull off a few cards from the top of the pack (say about six to twelve) while your right hand takes the main part of the pack over the top of the cards held by your

thumb. As soon as the right-hand cards are free, the cards in your left hand automatically drop into the palm and fingers of your left hand. Your left thumb is now free to slide another small batch of cards from the top of the pack in your right hand so that they fall onto the bunch in your left palm. Once the cards in your right hand are free again of the left, repeat the operation. When you've

done this five or six times, the remaining cards left in your right hand will be down to fewer than ten, and these you drop onto the cards in your left hand.

3 Repeat this operation three or four times and most will be satisfied that the cards are sufficiently rearranged.

This operation takes far longer to describe than to do – try it and practise it and you will master it in a very short time.

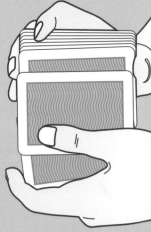

False overhand shuffles

False shuffles will enable you to keep a card or a group of cards on the top or bottom of the pack, or to transfer a card from the top to bottom or bottom to top of the pack while apparently mixing up the cards with the normal overhand shuffle.

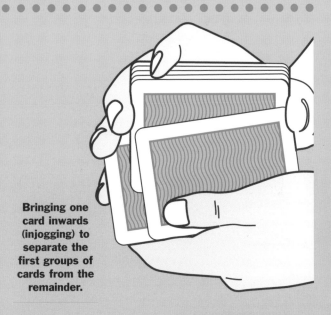

Bringing one card inwards (injogging) to separate the first groups of cards from the remainder.

False overhand shuffle 1

Let us say the King of Diamonds is at the top of the pack, and you want to shuffle the pack without disturbing its position.

Begin as for the normal shuffle, taking a few cards off the top of the pack with your left thumb and dropping them into your palm as you bring the larger part of the pack over the top.

This time you take only one card off the top of the main pack with your left thumb, and as you slide it onto the batch in your left palm you slide it inwards towards you, by say a centimetre or so. This card, called an injogged card, is now above the King of

Diamonds. You then proceed as before, so that at what would normally be the end of the shuffle the card above the King of Diamonds is sticking out of the pack towards you.

Of course, you do not want this to be obvious to the audience, so once the injogged card is in place, you carry on the shuffle by sliding the batches of cards into your left hand slightly unevenly. Only you will be aware of the injogged card.

The shuffle doesn't end here, however. As you

drop the last batch into your left hand, undercut the cards again by pushing upwards with your right thumb on the underside of the injogged card and bringing all the cards below it over the top and onto the pack again into the left hand. The King of Diamonds is back on top of the pack.

When you first try this with the cards in your hands you will find not only that you make mistakes, but that even when you get it right it looks clumsy, slow and unnatural to you. But with

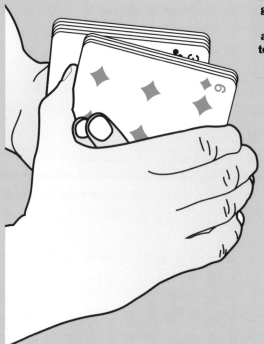

Pushing upwards on the injogged card to bring the groups of cards below it back over to the top again, thus retaining the top cards in their original position.

hand, the left-hand fingers keep hold of the bottom card. As your thumb pulls the top few cards from the pack they will fall onto the retained card, the Ace of Spades. You then complete the shuffle as normal. With practice, you will quickly be able to do this so fast that no one will notice, and even if they do they will think it is just part of a routine shuffle. But you will have the Ace of Spades where you want it on the bottom of the pack.

An alternative method is to shuffle the Ace to the top of the pack and then shuffle it to the bottom again. How to do this is explained in the two false shuffles that follow. Of course, this takes two operations, instead of one, but if you're more at ease with these shuffles, why not?

False overhand shuffle 3

Suppose you wanted to shuffle the King of Diamonds, which is at the top of the pack, to the

a little practice you will get it right. Remember – while another magician in the audience might notice what you're doing, he or she won't let on, just as you wouldn't if you were watching somebody else. To the rest of the audience you are merely shuffling the cards, and even when you fumble a little, just carry on – nobody else will probably notice.

This will work for any reasonable number of cards that you wish to retain at the top of the pack. All you have to do is ensure that the first batch of cards you withdraw with your left thumb is

large enough to include all the cards you wish to retain at the top. We will use this technique later in the book to keep the four Queens at the top of the pack and also in the trick called Clocking On.

False overhand shuffle 2

Suppose the vital card, the Ace of Spades, say, is at the bottom of the pack and you want to keep it there after you shuffle. With the cards in your left hand, press hard on the bottom card with your fingers. You carry on as for a normal overhand shuffle, but as you undercut with your right bottom. This is very simple. Hold the pack in your left hand in the normal shuffling position. Begin the shuffle by sliding just one card from the top of the pack into your left. In other words, your first undercut is of 51 cards. You then continue the shuffle as normal, finishing with the King of Diamonds on the bottom of the pack.

False overhand shuffle 4

It is just as easy to shuffle the bottom card to the top. All you do is execute the shuffle in the normal way, but make sure that the last 'batch' of cards pulled by the left thumb to the left hand consists of one card only. Just take care, as it is quite easy to slide the last two or three cards over at once, and if you do there's no going back, the trick will fail. So just keep going until you're sure there's only the one card in your right hand, which is, of course, the vital card.

False overhand shuffle 5

Sometimes you will have on top of the pack a card chosen by a member of the audience and which you will need to keep track of. This is done by peeking (see page 18) at the bottom card and then using this as a marker for the chosen card. With the cards in your left hand, pull off the top card and bring *all* of the rest of the cards over the top, in effect moving the top card to the bottom, so it is below your marker card. Without any hesitation, pull ten or so cards off with the left thumb and continue the shuffle in the normal way, taking care not to separate the bottom two cards, which will end near the top of the pack.

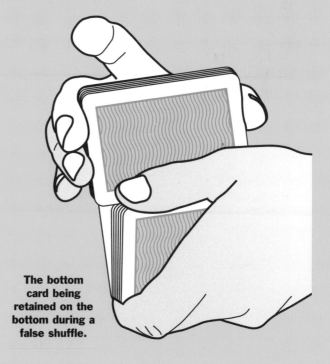

The bottom card being retained on the bottom during a false shuffle.

Repeat the normal shuffle, taking enough cards from the top of the pack to keep the two vital cards together, which will now switch to nearer the bottom. Now place the pack on the table and cut the pack by lifting about a third of the cards from the top. Complete the cut, and you will have the chosen card beneath your marker card somewhere near the middle of the pack.

False overhand shuffle 6

You might have a card at the top and a card at the bottom and wish either to switch them round or to keep them in the positions they are in. What you perform is a combination of false shuffles 3 and 4 above.

With the cards ready to shuffle in your left hand, begin by sliding just one card from the top with your left thumb as you undercut 51 cards. Carry on shuffling in the normal way until you have just two or three cards in your

right hand. Shuffle them one at a time. The essential thing is that the last batch consists of just one card (as the first batch did). You now have the original bottom card on top of the pack and the original top card on the bottom.

If you want the two cards back in their original positions, just repeat the above. This technique is used in the trick called It's all going wrong (see page 96).

False overhand shuffle 7

Sometimes you might want a group of cards at the bottom of the pack retained there, as with the trick called The upturned card (see page 59), where a group of five cards at the bottom of the pack must be retained there.

Shuffle in the normal way, but make sure that the last bundle carried over by the right hand is of a greater number of cards than those in question, in this case

five. As this bundle comes into the left hand, do not allow it to fall on the back of the cards already there, but use your left thumb to keep it separate. This bundle stays in your left hand, dropping into the palm as you take the remainder in your right hand and bring them back over into the left hand bundle by bundle. At the end, the original bottom cards are back on the bottom.

Sleights and shuffles

The glide

The glide is a very useful way of keeping the bottom card of the pack on the bottom while you are apparently dealing it to the table or handing it to the audience.

1 Suppose the Ace of Spades is the bottom card of the pack and you wish to persuade your audience that you are dealing it to the table. Hold the pack in your left hand with your thumb on one long side and your first three fingers along the other. Your little finger supports the pack as you show it to the audience (see top right).

2 Holding the cards lightly, turn your wrist to a palm-down position, at the same time moving your little finger onto the face of the bottom card. In the same movement, pull back the bottom card about a centimetre with the tips of your second and third fingers and your little finger too, if you find it helps (see bottom right). Practice will make

perfect. The most difficult thing is to pull back one card only. At first you will find perhaps two or three cards are being pulled back, but if your object is to merely retain the bottom card, this doesn't matter. However, it is best

The Ace of Spades shown to the audience as the bottom card of the pack.

to practise until you are sure you can move back the bottom card only, exposing the tip of the second-bottom card (in this case the five of Diamonds).

3 With the bottom card (the Ace of Spades) pulled back, your right fingertips pull the five of Diamonds from the 'bottom' of the pack, which you lay face down on the table. Now slide the bottom card back level with the rest, and you have apparently dealt the Ace of Spades to the table while in fact keeping it where you want it – at the bottom of the pack.

View from behind the magician's hand showing the second and third fingers gliding back the bottom card, enabling the second-bottom card to be dealt.

Sleights and shuffles

15

The double lift

The double lift is a very useful way of keeping a card which you wish to disguise from the audience at the top of a face-down pack. By showing the audience the *second* card as if it were the top one you can keep the identity of the top card secret. There are two methods of executing the double lift.

Double lift 1

1 First you need to make a break between the top two cards of the pack and the rest with your little finger. You can do this while talking to the audience by holding the pack in your left hand and dreamily fanning it out with your right. As you do so your hand takes the top two cards far enough out to the right to that when you square up the cards you can get the little finger of your left hand underneath the corner of the second card (see top right). As you square up the cards with your right hand, with your palm down, the thumb at the bottom of the pack and your second and third fingers at the top, you are hiding from the audience the fact that your little finger is inserted a little way into the pack.

2 Now bend your right index finger so that it is pressing on the top card, and lift the top two cards with your right thumb. Your thumb pushes the top two cards forward slightly, allowing you to straighten your left little finger, which has now done its job. As the two cards move forward, the second and third fingers of your right hand lift the top two cards as one and your index finger keeps the two cards bent and exactly aligned with

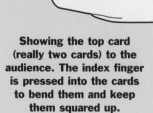

The little-finger break, showing the little finger separating the two top cards from the rest of the pack.

Showing the top card (really two cards) to the audience. The index finger is pressed into the cards to bend them and keep them squared up.

each other (see above). Show the card (which is actually the second card) to the audience, and return both of them to the pack, squaring the pack up.

Sleights and shuffles

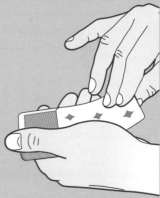

Double-lifting the top cards with the help of the second and third fingers of the left hand.

Double lift 2

This way of doing the double lift requires the same little-finger break.

1 Again you push the two top cards forward a centimetre or two with your right thumb, releasing your left little finger. While this is happening your right index finger is pressing down on the two cards as before and your left thumb comes over the pack as if it is pushing the top card to your right. At the same time, your left index finger is holding the rest of the pack back while the second and third fingers of your left hand are holding the long sides of the two cards and with the help of the left thumb are helping to keep the two cards lined up. Your right-hand fingers and thumbs are keeping the cards lined up top and bottom (see top right).

2 You can now let go with your right hand and grasp the two cards at the top between your right thumb and two first fingers (see right). Turn the two cards over and lay them on top of the face-down pack, slightly overlapping at the top (see bottom right).

Grasping the top two cards between fingers and thumb.

3 When the audience has satisfied themselves as to the 'top' card, pick the two cards up together and return them face down onto the pack, squaring it up and deceiving your audience nicely. Of course, you must make sure that the top two cards are exactly aligned at all times. The whole operation is much simpler to do than to describe, and if you follow the directions carefully and practise, you will soon be able to double-lift smoothly and convincingly.

Laying top two cards face up on the pack, overlapping at the top to show the audience the 'top' card. Without changing your grip, you can now lay them back down on the pack, with the five of Diamonds the second card down.

Peeking

In many tricks when you are trying to locate a spectator's card, it is necessary to know the bottom card of the pack. Clearly you cannot openly look at the bottom card, so you have to find ways of peeking without making your audience suspicious.

1 If you have the pack in your right hand, you can square it up by holding it with your thumb and fingers on the short sides and tapping one long side on the table. As you do so a casual glance at what you're doing will allow a split-second peek at the bottom card.

2 As you are talking to the audience, perhaps telling them what the next trick is called, hold the cards in your right hand, with the palm facing slightly downwards and the bottom card facing towards your left shoe. Your right thumb is grasping the cards' short side nearest to you, your second and third fingers are holding the other short side, and your index finger is on the centre of the top card.

3 As you talk, make that gesture common to television reporters when explaining something – open your arms slightly while turning your palms half-upwards. Do this in a way in which the pack in your right hand is turned towards you, so that with a quick and casual peek you can see the bottom card. Then turn the palms downward again. Having finished your explanation place the cards in your left hand and shuffle them, using false shuffle 2 (see page 12) which keeps the bottom card on the bottom where you want it.

Getting a quick peek at the bottom card.

TIP
When taking the cards back from a spectator who has just shuffled them, take the pack in your right hand with the palm facing down. As you transfer the pack to your left hand before the next stage of the trick, tilt the pack slightly so that you get a peek at the bottom card.

Palming

Palming is one of those sleight-of-hand skills that, when you first try them, seem very difficult to accomplish. However, you will find that practice brings improvement very quickly and soon you can palm a card with confidence.

1 Palming means to take a card or cards from the top of the pack without the audience knowing, or to add a card or cards to the pack without being seen.

2 With the pack in your left hand, bring your right hand over as if squaring up the cards. As your right hand covers the cards from the audience's view, use your left thumb to push the top card slightly to the right, so that the top right-hand corner of the card is pressed firmly against the top joint of the little finger of your right hand. Your left thumb can then swivel the card into your right palm, while your second and third fingers can push the centre of the card upwards so that it bends and follows the contours of your palm, with the bottom of the card resting against the ball of your thumb.

3 With the card resting snugly in your palm, do not be in too much of a hurry to remove your right hand. As you withdraw the pack from the cover of your right hand, continue to use the fingers of your right hand to square the cards. Then slowly let your right hand drop to your side, keeping the palmed card from your audience, of course. If needed, you can casually slip the palmed card into your pocket at a convenient moment.

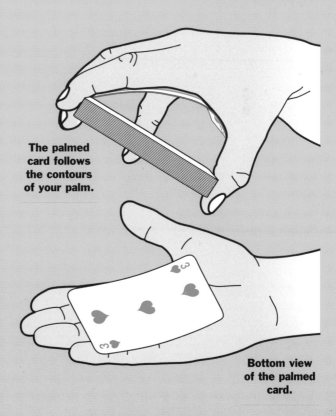

The palmed card follows the contours of your palm.

Bottom view of the palmed card.

Forcing

Occasionally for a trick to work you need to force a card or cards on to a spectator (let's call her Rachael) so that she thinks that she has chosen the card entirely at random. Here are two ways to force a card.

Criss-cross force

You want to force a member of the audience to select a card whose identity you know.

The criss-cross force is one way of doing it, but you must do it quickly and confidently, with diverting patter if you can manage it. If somebody has time to analyse what you are doing, they will realize that the card which has been 'freely' chosen was actually the top one of the pack.

1 First take a peek (see page 18) at the bottom card of the pack as you casually square it up. Do not let Rachael see it, as it is the one she is going to choose quite freely! Let's say the bottom card is the Jack of Diamonds.

2 Give the cards one or three false shuffles to move the Jack of Diamonds to the top (see page 11). Now place the pack on the table and ask Rachael to cut the pack by taking off the top half and placing it on the table. Pick up the bottom half and place it crossways on top of the other.

3 Now you need some misdirection. Say 'OK, you could have cut the pack anywhere, correct?' Rachael agrees. 'And I gave the pack a good shuffle before you cut it?' Rachael agrees again. 'So there's no way I can know your card?' As you say this, lift off the half of the pack that is resting on the other, point to the top card of the half that remains, and say 'OK, look at it then and without me seeing, show it to the others'.

4 Next say to Rachael 'Remember what the card is, put it back into the pack and (handing Rachael the rest of the pack) shuffle all the cards together so that it is completely lost in the pack'. Well, so it is – but you know Rachael's chosen card is the Jack of Diamonds.

Double-turnover force

Again, by some means you need to know the top card of the pack.

Here again, when you perform to yourself in practice the double-turnover force, you will think 'Of course, it's obvious that the chosen card is the one originally on top of the pack'. So you must perform it so that nobody in the audience has time to think the same thing. You have the advantage that the audience hasn't seen the move before and they'll be too interested in what you will be doing next to try to work out what exactly you've already done.

1 Give the pack a false shuffle (see page 11) making sure the card you want to force remains on the top. Let's say it's the seven of Hearts.

2 Hold the pack out face down to one of the audience, say Freddie, and say 'Take a few cards off the top, Freddie, and put them back face up.' Freddie does. 'Thank you, Freddie, now would somebody else, perhaps you Alice, take a larger cut from the top and put the lot back face up.' Alice does. In your hand now you have a pack of which the top part is face up and the bottom part face down.

3 Fan through the cards until you hold all the face-up cards in your right hand and ask Alice to take the top face-down card from your left hand. Say 'That's the card which Freddie and you have chosen from a shuffled and twice-cut pack.' It seems to the audience as if this must be a card chosen at random – only you know it is the seven of Hearts.

You can use this shuffle to force a group of cards, as in the trick of Memorizing the telephone book (see page 74).

The roly-poly pass

The roly-poly pass is not exactly a shuffle or a cut but it is a very useful device when you use it together with a false shuffle. When you have asked a spectator to select a card and then return it to the middle of the pack to be 'lost', this manoeuvre allows you to keep the card just where you want it.

1 Once the spectator has taken a card, cut the pack at the point where the spectator took his card, and square up the two piles, holding the bottom half of the pack face down in your left hand and the top half in your right. Ask the spectator to place his card on your left-hand pile.

2 Bring the top half of the pack across, placing its left edge just below the right edge of the bottom half (see below). Using the right-hand half of the pack gently flip the bottom half over so that it is face up in your left hand (see opposite, top).

3 At the same time, turn over the top half of the pack and drop it face up onto the bottom half (see opposite, bottom).

4 This manoeuvre should result in all of the cards being face up in the palm of your left hand, and your right hand, without leaving your left hand, can pull the pack over, face down, onto your left fingers in the position to begin a shuffle.

5 The spectator's card is now on top of the pack, and without

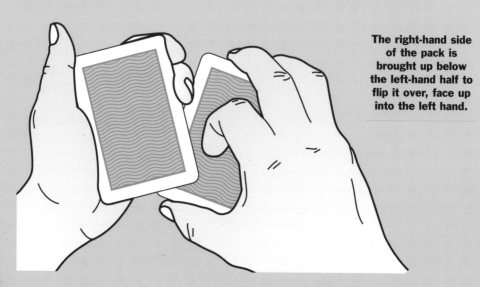

The right-hand side of the pack is brought up below the left-hand half to flip it over, face up into the left hand.

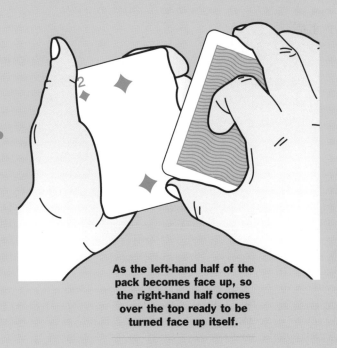

separating your hands you can go straight into a false shuffle. If you use false shuffle 3 (see page 12) you can take the card to the bottom of the pack, and continuing straight into false shuffle 4 (see page 13) you can have the chosen card top of the pack again.

As the left-hand half of the pack becomes face up, so the right-hand half comes over the top ready to be turned face up itself.

6 This description sounds complicated and if you go through the moves slowly you will think it very clumsy. But if you practise you will see in a few minutes that in fact you can do it very quickly.

The right index finger reaches over the pile in the right hand turning it face up as it puts it onto the pile in the left hand. In one movement the right hand flips the whole pack face down into the fingers of the left hand and begins a false shuffle.

7 The roly-poly pass will look to the audience like a normal way of beginning a shuffle, and if you go immediately in the same movement into a shuffle nobody will question it at all.

8 The roly-poly pass with false shuffles is used to good effect in the trick called The wrong card (see page 115).

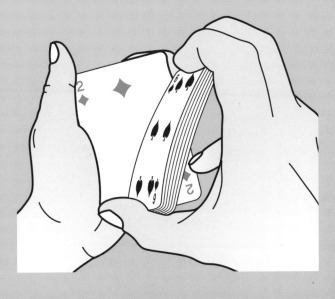

Simple
tricks

In this section are some simple tricks which
you can master quickly. Performing them
successfully will give you confidence. You do
not need any of the special sleights, and
some are mathematical tricks which work
themselves. However, all need care and
self-confidence to perform well.

An improved memory trick

You will need
A standard pack.

The trick
A spectator picks a card from 21 offered, remembers it and returns it to the pack, which is shuffled. The magician three times deals the pack face up into three piles, the spectator each time indicating in which pack his card is. The magician then reveals the card.

How to do it
This is about the simplest card trick I know – you hardly have to do anything and it works itself. It could easily be done by a seven-year-old, but is worth considering as a way of showing how easy it is to improve tricks by adding your own little touches to make them fresher and force people who think they know how it is done to think a little harder.

1 In the basic trick as children know it, any 21 cards are counted from the top of the pack – these are all that will be used. Ask one of your audience, say Tom, to shuffle the cards and to pick out one to remember. This card should be shown to the rest of the audience but not to you and then inserted among the other 20 and the pack shuffled.

2 Now hold the pack face down in one hand and deal the cards with the other into three piles of seven cards, face up. As you do so you tell Tom to watch out for his card and at the end to let you know which pile it is in. You then join the three piles together making sure that the pile with the chosen card in it is placed in the centre between the other two piles. You then deal the pack out again into three piles and ask again in which pile is the chosen card. Again this pile goes in between the other two piles when you pick them up and then for the third and last time you deal the three piles as before, and again put the chosen pile between the other two. You then begin to deal the cards into one pile, silently counting to ten as you go, and when you lay down the eleventh card you say 'This is your card.'

The drawback of the trick is that anyone seeing it even for the first time might well spot that you are placing the pile with the chosen card in it in between the other two piles. They will notice immediately if you always pick up the selected pile first and then clumsily put one pile above and the other below it. So the first task is to try to disguise this as naturally as possible. I suggest the best way is as follows:

● If the selected pile is the centre one, slide the right-hand pile off the table, place it on the centre pile, slide these

Simple tricks

SUGGESTED VERSION

This is how I think this trick can be played most effectively.
After you have dealt the three piles for the first time, and you
know which pile Tom's card is in, pick them up casually. At the
same time distract the audience by explaining that by trying to
remember which cards are in the pile selected you propose to
reveal the chosen card. So while dealing the cards out into three
piles study the cards as if you're trying to remember them. After
the third deal, when you know the chosen card, pick up the piles
and casually shuffle them. Anybody who thinks they know the
trick will now be amazed and think you've slipped up. Hand them
to Tom and ask him to shuffle them and spread them face up on
the table while you concentrate. With the 21 cards on the table,
pore over them for a few seconds, say that you've narrowed it
down to two, and then say with a worried look that you'll settle
for this one, and pick up the chosen card. Look relieved and
pleased when you are right and accept the congratulations.
You deserve them, you've made a simple mechanical trick a
little more interesting.

two piles together off the table and place them on the left-hand pile. Then slide all three off the table.

● If the selected pile is the right-hand pile, slide it off the table, place it on the centre pile, slide the combined pile off the table and into your left hand, then slide the left-hand pile off the table and place it on top.

● If the selected pile is the left-hand pile, slide it off the table, place it on the centre pile and slide the new pile off the table into your left hand, then place the right-hand pile on top.

Double prediction

Skill level 1

You will need
A standard pack.

The trick
The pack is shuffled by a spectator. The magician then fans through the pack to extract two Aces, which are given to two spectators. The magician deals the pack face down until the first spectator says 'Stop.' He inserts his Ace face up on the pile, the magician makes the pack whole again and repeats the operation, with the second spectator inserting her Ace face up where she says 'Stop.' The magician then deals through the pack to the two face-up Aces, each time predicting the card above the Ace.

How to do it

1 Hand the pack to a member of the audience to shuffle. When taking it back, say 'I'll need two marker cards, a couple of Aces will do.' Fan through the cards, take out two Aces and lay them face up on the table. While doing this, notice and remember the cards on the top and the bottom of the pack. Let's assume it's the six of Clubs on top and the King of Hearts on the bottom. Don't allow anybody else to see the top card of the pack. Hand the Aces to two members of the audience – let's call them Jamie and Phoebe.

2 With the pack face down in your left hand, begin dealing the cards face down on the table with your right hand. Ask Jamie to call 'stop' at any point. When he does so, ask him to place his Ace face up on top of the pile, then place the rest of the cards from your hand face down on top of it. Pick up the whole pack again and tell the audience that you are going to predict the two cards where Jamie and Phoebe will call 'stop' Start dealing again face down onto the table, asking Phoebe to call 'stop' whenever she pleases. When she does, ask her to place her Ace face up on top of the pile. You then put the rest of the pack face down on top of it as before.

3 After pretending to concentrate, pick up the pack from the table and, holding it face down, fan through it to the first face-up Ace. Holding the cards above the Ace in your right hand, say 'Jamie, I think you cut the pack at the six of Clubs.' Lay the pile in your right hand face up on the table and the top card will be the six of Clubs.

4 Lay the face-up Ace beside it on the table and fan through the cards until you come to the second face-up Ace. With an expression of deep thought on your face, say 'And I think, Phoebe, that you cut the cards at the King of Hearts.' Again lay down the cards in your right hand face up and the top card will be the King of Hearts.

TIP

It may happen that the second person you ask to call 'stop', in this case Phoebe, in a sly attempt to mess you up, will allow you to deal cards past the first upturned Ace. It doesn't matter, but at the end, when you fan the cards down to the first Ace, you must alter your patter a little. The first Ace will now be the one next to Phoebe's card, so you must deal with her first. You say 'Phoebe, I think you cut the pack at the King of Hearts' and, as before, lay down the pile face up in your right hand. The top card will be the King of Hearts. Lay the Ace beside it and fan down to the second Ace. This time Jamie's card will be the card below it. Now lay the cards in your right hand face down on the table. Remove the face-up Ace from the top of the pile in your left hand, place that on the table and say 'Jamie, you cut the cards at the six of Clubs', turning over the top card in your left hand, which will be the six of Clubs.

If Phoebe should decide to be really awkward, and say 'stop' as soon as Jamie's Ace is laid on the table, all the better. Ask her to lay her Ace on top of Jamie's and place the rest of the pack on top. Say 'So you thought you'd mess me about and cut the cards at the same place. Well it won't work. I think you both put your Ace between the six of Clubs and King of Hearts.' Pick up the pack, fan through to the two Aces and lay the pile in your right hand face up on the table to reveal the King of Hearts. Take the two Aces from the top of the pile in your left hand, lay them on the table, and then turn over the top card of the pile that's left and reveal it to be the six of Clubs. You're entitled to look a bit cocky as you say 'You can't fool me.'

The four burglars

Skill level 1

You will need
A standard pack.

The trick
The audience are shown the four Jacks, which are placed on top of the pack. They are said to be burglars, while the pack represents a mansion to be robbed. The first Jack is propped against an object on a glass table. He represents a lookout in the garden. The second Jack is placed on the bottom of the pack to search the basement. The third is placed in the middle of the pack to search the dining rooms, etc, while the fourth is inserted near the top of the pack to search the bedrooms. At a signal from the lookout in the garden, the Jacks all rush to the roof to hide, and are found back on top of the pack.

How to do it
This was the first trick I was ever shown as a child more than 60 years ago, and this is more or less as I first knew it, a very simple trick but with an entertaining story.

1 You could begin with a prepared pack, but it is not difficult to rig the pack while idly playing with it before the trick, or while starting your patter. 'For this trick,' you say, 'I need the four Jacks, also known with reason as knaves, because they are very naughty rascals, especially when they get together, and are not above a little criminal activity.'

2 While you are saying this, search the pack for the Jacks, but at the same time arrange the pack to get the sequence Jack, Jack, Jack, three plain cards, Jack at the top. Fan them out with the ordinary cards hidden behind the third Jack so that you can show them to the audience as four Jacks (see above). Place the rest of the pack face down on the table.

The fan of four Jacks as shown to the audience, with three ordinary cards between the third and fourth Jacks. Of course, the audience only sees four Jacks and do not suspect the hidden cards.

3 Say 'One dark night the four Jacks proposed to rob a rich mansion, their original plan being to gain access to the roof via the fire escape and make their way in through the fanlight. The pack here represents the mansion, with the four burglars on the roof.' You fold the fan and place it face down on top of the pack. The second, third and fourth cards on the top of the pack are not Jacks, of course.

4 Continue 'But they had a change of plan, realizing that it would be better if one of them stayed in the garden as a lookout, in case the law should appear. So one of the burglars didn't make his way to the roof, he stayed in the garden and kept watch.'

5 Take the top card from the pack, a Jack, and prop it against any object (a wine glass, for example) on the table. 'He's the lookout' you say.

6 'The other Jacks went to the roof and followed the original plan. The first went down to the basement to look around and see what he could find.' Place the top card near the bottom of the pack (it is not, of course, a Jack). 'The next Jack went down to the dining room, library and general living rooms.' Place the third card in the centre of the pack. 'And the final Jack searched the bedrooms, looking for jewellery, etc.' Place the fourth card about a quarter of the way down from the top of the pack.

● ● ● ● ● ● ● ● ● ● ● ● ● ● ● ●

7 Now tell your audience 'While everybody was stealthily going about their business, a policeman came wandering up the road and stopped in front of the mansion, and began to stroll up the drive as if to check that everything was OK. The Jack in the garden...' (indicate the Jack on the table) '...decided it was risky enough to issue a warning. So he whistled.' If you are a good whistler give a loud whistle. This will add amusement to your performance.

8 'At this all the Jacks rushed up to the roof prior to making their escape down the fire escape.' Riffle the pack. 'And here they are – all on the roof.' Turn over the top three cards to reveal that they are the other three Jacks.

IMPROVEMENT

As I said, this is the original trick, needing no special sleight-of-hand skills. However, if you have mastered the double lift, and are not happy about the way you have to arrange the pack at the beginning, you can get your four Jacks to the top of the pack by the method described in the trick called The four aces (see page 100). It is used also in another trick involving the four Jacks, entitled Jumping jacks (see page 93).

On the other hand, suppose you perform the Jumping jacks trick first. While collecting the Jacks after that trick, you can arrange them in the fan as shown on the previous page and can then go straight into the Four burglars trick. Having seen you just use the Jacks, the audience will be less inclined to be suspicious of your opening fan of 'four Jacks'. Your initial patter will need to be different 'Now you know what these terrible Jacks can do, let me tell you about a nasty crime they nearly got away with a little while ago...'

Tricky band

Skill level 2

You will need
A standard pack, an elastic band big enough to wrap around the pack quite tightly, without the danger of it snapping or damaging the cards.

The trick
A spectator picks and memorizes a card. An elastic band is placed round the pack, and the spectator inserts his card into the pack. Another spectator twangs the elastic band, the band is removed, and the chosen card is found to have turned over.

How to do it

1 Fan out the cards and ask somebody from the audience, say Joe, to extract any card of his choice and, without showing you, to show what it is to the rest of the audience.

2 For this trick you need the card at the face-up end of the pack to be turned over, so that the pack appears to be face down, whichever end you view it from. If this is the first trick you perform, you can prepare the pack in advance. Otherwise, you must achieve this without suspicion, either by casually turning the card in a break for chattering or during the trick itself, i.e. by telling your audience you will turn your back for a second while Joe shows the card round. It is simplest to turn over the top card of the pack then turn the whole pack over. When you present the pack to Joe again, the pack is actually face up, except for the top card.

The magician holds the pack with the elastic band round it, while the spectator inserts his chosen card.

3 You now produce the elastic band and ask Joe or, even better, somebody else, say Emily, to place the elastic band over the pack. You then ask Joe to insert his card face down in the centre of the pack. It should be as near as possible to the centre, as the pack will be turned over before Joe's card is revealed, so it will be obvious if Joe inserted his card near the bottom and it turned out later to be near the top. It is best to use cards that have a white border round the backs, so that it is impossible for Joe to notice that he is placing his card between two face-up cards.

4 Now comes the hardest part of the trick, the misdirection. Dropping your left hand, which holds the cards, to your side, say 'What I am going to do is make Joe's card turn over.' Add with emphasis, if necessary pointing your finger at your audience so that they look at your face 'Or rather, *you* are going to do it.' While you are saying this, bring your left hand, which is holding the cards palm down, up to your right hand and place the cards in your right hand, absent-mindedly squaring them up. You have effectively turned the pack over, so that the whole pack – except the bottom card and Joe's card – is face down.

MOVING TO THE NEXT TRICK

Because the bottom card of the pack is also face up, it is a bit awkward to go straight on to your next trick. The best way to put this right is as follows. When you fan down to Joe's card, take the cards above it in your right hand, flipping them face up. This is quite a natural thing to do, because with your left thumb you now push Joe's card onto the other face-up cards in your right hand. Look at the audience rather than the cards as you make the pack whole by putting the face-down cards in your left hand on top of the face-up cards in your right hand, making it look as if you are doing it absent-mindedly. Somebody in the audience might point out your error, in which case you say 'Silly me' and put the pack to rights. If nobody notices, spot it yourself before you begin your next trick and with a look of irritation put the cards right. Although you seem to have made a silly mistake in getting one half of the pack face up and the other one face down, what you've actually done is corrected the odd card that was facing the wrong way.

● ● ● ● ● ● ● ● ● ● ● ● ● ● ● ●

5 You then say 'Now who is likely to have the most magical touch? Perhaps you, Emily. Would you kindly twang the elastic band for me.' Emily does, and you transfer the pack to your left hand, making it very clear this time that you are not turning the pack over. With your right hand you take off the elastic band and fan through the cards. Near the middle, there will be Joe's card face up. You say 'Well done, Emily. I take it this was your chosen card, Joe?' Joe admits that it was, and you proceed quickly to your next trick. Make sure you fan well past Joe's card, so that the audience can see that it is the only one that is face up. But don't fan right to the bottom of the pack because if you do that you will reveal the bottom card as well.

Five-finger exercise

Skill level 1

You will need
A standard pack.

The trick
A spectator fans out her fingers on the table as if playing the piano. Two cards are placed between each pair of fingers and finger and thumb on her left hand. Two cards are similarly placed between each pair of fingers on her right hand, but the space between finger and thumb has only one card. The pairs of cards are split up, with one dealt to one pile and the second on the other. The spectator is allowed to put the odd card onto whichever pile she likes. But amazingly, the magician makes the odd card change piles.

• •

How to do it
This is a simple trick which works itself. If you perform it, do so early and pass on quickly to another trick, because the observer will work it out if given time for a little thought.

1 Ask an onlooker, let's call her Karen, to spread her fingers on the table so that you can stand pairs of cards up between them. Beginning with the space between the little and third fingers of her left hand, place two cards, asking her to close up her fingers to hold the cards upright. Continue along the left hand, putting two cards between each pair of fingers, finally placing two between the index finger and thumb. Repeat the procedure with the right hand, but when you reach the gap between right index finger and thumb, place one card there only, pointing out to all that there is only one card.

Simple tricks

2 Say 'What I am now going to do is take each pair of cards in turn, and put one in one pile and one in another.' Begin by taking the cards from between the left little and third fingers and putting one on the left and the other on the right, saying 'Here's a pair.' Take the next two cards and add them to the piles, saying 'Here's another pair.'

3 By the time you get to the odd card at the end, the one between right index finger and thumb, there will be two piles of cards before you. Say to Karen 'Now there's only the one odd card left. Which pile would you like to put it on? You can place it on whichever pile you wish.'

4 Karen will place the odd card on one of the piles – it does not matter which. Now say, indicating the pile on which Karen placed the last card, 'We have the odd card on this pile. What I am going to do, with my hidden resources of magic, is to transfer the odd card to the other pile.'

5 Tap the top of the pile containing the odd card and mutter any little incantation, then pick up the pile and deal it into two piles, as you did before, saying 'Here's a pair, here's a pair', and so on. Strangely, the odd card will be found to have disappeared.

6 Say 'It worked. The odd card has gone. The only thing to check now is whether it really did go to the other column.' Pick up the other pile and count them out in pairs as before. Oddly, you will find that at the end you have one card left. Say 'Ah, there it is. There are still some unexplainable mysteries left in the world...'

EXPLANATION

If you think about it, you will see that as there are 19 cards in total, the pile without the extra card will contain only nine cards, while Karen's chosen pile will contain ten.

Simple tricks

Matching cuts

Skill level 2

You will need
A standard pack.

The trick
A spectator shuffles the pack. The magician takes it and chooses three prediction cards, laying them on the table as cards that will predict the cards exposed by a spectator's three cuts. The spectator makes two cuts, in effect dividing the pack into three parts. The three cards exposed by these cuts are shown to match in rank and colour the three prediction cards extracted beforehand.

How to do it
This is a trick which uses the same deceptive cut as Double prediction (see page 29), so perhaps it would be best not to do both tricks in the same routine. This one requires no special sleights.

1 Give the pack to one of the audience, say Chloe. Tell Chloe to give the pack a good shuffle and then take it. Say you are going to predict three cards which Chloe will later pick of her own free will, so you need to take out three cards to indicate your predictions. Tell Chloe that magicians call them prediction cards.

2 Turn the pack so that you are looking at the faces of the cards, but make sure the audience cannot see them. First of all note the top card of the face-up pack, i.e. the card to the right as you look at them. Let us say it is the ten of Clubs. Fan out the cards – first of all you are looking for the ten of Spades, i.e. the card of the same rank and colour of the card you've noted. Take out the ten of Spades and lay it face down on the table before you. Say 'This is my first prediction card.'

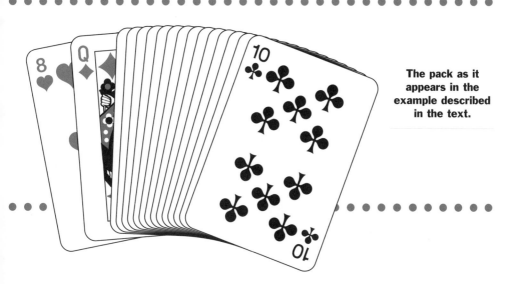

The pack as it appears in the example described in the text.

3 Continue to fan the cards until you can see which two cards are at the bottom of the face-up pack. Let us say the eight of Hearts is at the bottom, with the Queen of Diamonds next to it. Fan back through the pack. You are looking now for the eight of Diamonds and Queen of Hearts.

4 Suppose first you came to the Queen of Hearts. Take this card out and lay it face down to the right of the card already on the table. Continue fanning until you come to the eight of Diamonds and place it face down on the table to the left. The order in which you take these two cards does not matter, but you must place them on the table in the same order as their equivalents in the pack as you are looking at it. For example the match for the bottom card of the pack goes on the left of the original card and the match for the second-bottom card goes on the right.

5 While doing this, do not let your audience get any clues as to how you are selecting your prediction cards. Pretend you are giving the matter a certain amount of thought, for example 'I think the second card might be a red one and quite a high one, a picture card perhaps.'

6 When the three cards are in place, square up the pack and say to Chloe 'Now you'll notice I didn't alter the order of the cards in any way after you'd shuffled them. What you must do now is cut the cards wherever you like and I am predicting that the cards at the places where you cut them will correspond to the three cards I have laid down as prediction cards.'

Simple tricks

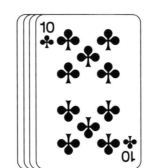

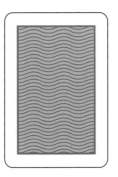
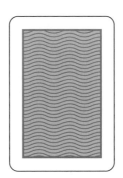
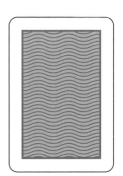

How the layout on the table will look at the end of the trick before the face-down cards are exposed. The top cards of the piles will be eight of Hearts, ten of Clubs (already exposed), Queen of Diamonds. The three cards below are the eight of Diamonds, ten of Spades and Queen of Hearts.

7 Lay the pack in your hand face down on the table and say to Chloe 'What you must do first is cut the cards by taking a pile off the top of the pack – not too many because you've got to cut again afterwards.'

8 Chloe will take a few cards from the top. Say to her 'Now lay the cards in your hand face up on top of the pile on the table.' When she's done this, say to her 'Now cut again, taking a larger number of cards from the top.' When Chloe has done this tell her to put them down on the table, and then say to her 'Now pick up the cards that are left and place them face down on top.'

9 When she's done this say 'Excellent' and pick up the pack, turning it over. 'What we have here now is a pack that is made up of face-up cards, then face-down cards with more face-up cards on the bottom. And the cards change from face down to face up at the places where you have freely cut them, Chloe. What we must do now is see how well and how many times the cards at the places where you cut correspond to the cards that I predicted.'

As you speak, you can fan out the cards slightly to show Chloe and the audience that indeed you have face-up cards at both ends of the pack with face-down cards in the centre.

10 Now fan down the pack till you come to the first face-down card. Take all the face-up cards above it into your right hand and, turning the pile over, lay them face down on the table next to the prediction card on the left. Now take off the top face-down card held in your

left hand and place it face down on top of the pile you've just set down. Tap the new top card on this pile and say 'This is your cut which corresponds to the first prediction card.'

11 Now take in your right hand all the face-down cards from the remainder of the pack still in your left hand, leaving only the face-up cards in your left hand (in this case headed by the ten of Clubs).

12 Place the face-up pile next to the centre card on the table, saying 'This corresponds to the centre prediction card.' Then lay the face-down cards in your right hand face down next to the right-hand prediction card, saying 'And this cut corresponds to the right-hand prediction card.' See above left for how the table should look. Continue by saying 'Now, Chloe, how well do you think I might have done with my predictions? One right will be good, but I'm hoping for at least two. Please turn over the top card in this pile.' You point to the left-hand pile. Chloe turns over the eight of Hearts. You turn over your prediction card. It is the eight of Diamonds.

13 'Well, that's fantastic, and to be honest, a bit of a relief. Now we know the second card you cut to was the ten of Clubs, so let's see what my prediction was.' You turn over the centre prediction card. It is the ten of Spades.

14 You say 'I am now perfectly satisfied. If I get three right I might come among you with a hat so that you can show your appreciation. Please turn over your third card, Chloe.'

15 Chloe exposes the Queen of Diamonds. You turn over your card – the Queen of Hearts. Look very satisfied with yourself as you collect up the cards.

Boxing clever

Skill level 2

You will need
A boxed pack of cards, a clean handkerchief, pencil and paper.

The trick
The magician takes a boxed pack of cards from the table, opens the box and removes the cards. Handing them to a spectator, he asks the spectator to shuffle the cards thoroughly and then lay them out in a line of seven piles on the table. He then gives the spectator the pencil and paper and asks him to write down a column of numbers from one to seven, circling one of the numbers – any one of his choice. The magician looks at the top card of each pile, and states what the card is, the spectator writing it down against the pile number on his list. The spectator collects up all the piles into one pack and shuffles them thoroughly. He then puts the pack on the table and cuts it into two. The magician puts the card box on top of one half of the pack, and asks the spectator to put the other half on top of that. The magician covers the whole with the handkerchief and taps the top of the column beneath. He then removes the handkerchief, asks the spectator to take the half-pack above the card box and another to take the half below and to search through them for the seven cards listed on the paper. Six of the cards are soon found, but the card that was circled has disappeared. A third spectator is asked to pick up the box and shake it. It rattles. She is then asked to look inside. She takes out the missing card.

How to do it

1 Take up a boxed pack of cards. The box itself is to be used in the trick, which is why it is necessary to use a different pack. The box might contain a pack you have used for an earlier trick, which indicates to the audience that it has not been prepared. Your first little deception is to leave the bottom card of the pack in the box, at the same time noting what it is. This is not as easy as it sounds. I suggest opening the box with its flap away from you, i.e. obstructing the audience's view. Holding the box in your left hand, tip the cards half out of the box into your right hand. Grab most of the cards between your right thumb and fingers, at the same time tilting the box upright again, and making sure that a small number remain in the box. This often will happen naturally, but if

1	4C
2	QH
3	7C
4	KD
⑤	9D
6	
7	

● ●

The helper is writing the card at the top of each pile against the number of the pile. When he reaches the circled number, he is given the name of the card remaining in the box, in this case the nine of Diamonds.

necessary push a few back with your fingers. Lay the majority of the pack on the table and then retrieve the missing few from the box.

Keeping the box upright, it is now comparatively easy to take out the few cards left while leaving the bottom card there. My method is to tip the box, and therefore the cards, forward while holding the bottom card back with the middle finger. The first finger and thumb extract the cards, and you can easily see which card is left. Let us suppose it is the nine of Diamonds.

2 Place the last few cards with the rest of the pack, close the flap of the box (safely holding the nine of Diamonds) and set it to one side.

3 Hand the pack to your helper, say Samuel, and ask him to shuffle well and make the line of seven piles. Give him the pencil and paper and ask him to write down the numbers one to seven and to circle his choice of number. Note which number he circles.

4 You then tell Samuel he is to write against his numbers the top card of each pile, which you will read out to him. Look at the top card of the pile at one end and read it out. Now, if Samuel laid out his piles left to right as you look at them, and his circled number is five, begin with the pile on your left, calling it pile 1. If his circled number is two, begin with the pile on your right, calling it pile 7. The object of this is to make the pile that is circled appear later rather than sooner in the calling out. In other words, if the circled number is 4, 5, 6 or 7, begin calling out the piles at 1. If it is 1, 2, or 3, make the first card you call out pile 7. It is important that the audience

The pack divided into two halves, with the box (containing the missing card) between them, covered by the magician's handkerchief.

♣ ◇ P L A Y I N G ♡ ♠
C A R D S

doesn't expect you to show them the actual cards on top of the piles, because on one occasion you are going to deceive them again.

5 Let us assume Samuel circled the number five on his list. You can therefore begin your calling out at pile 1. Lift up the card and identify it, saying, for example 'Pile number one is the four of Clubs.' Hold the card for a second or two while Samuel writes it down, casually allowing the audience to see that you are calling it correctly, but without actually showing it to them. Replace it on the pile. Read out the card on pile two similarly. With the card on pile three replace it a little more quickly without the audience seeing it. Make sure Samuel has written it down before picking up the next card, which you can replace quite quickly. The audience is now used to you not actually showing the cards, and as they do not know yet the purpose of the writing down, will not

question you. If they do, you must say something like 'Patience – we're coming to that.'

6 When you come to pile 5, Samuel's circled number, you look at the card on top of the pile, but you call out the card in the box, i.e. the nine of Diamonds.

7 When Samuel has written down all seven cards, ask him to pick up all the piles into one pack again, and give them a thorough shuffle. Then ask him to place them on the table and cut them into two piles.

8 Taking the box, ask Samuel which pile he would like the box placed on. Place it on his choice, then ask him to put the other pile on top of the box.

Simple tricks

9 Produce a clean handkerchief from your pocket and lay it on the column formed by the cards and box. Say to the audience 'I am now going to perform an interesting experiment', and tap the top of the column through the handkerchief with your fingers. Say 'That should do it' and remove the handkerchief.

10 Say to Samuel 'Would you take the pile of cards above the box, Samuel, and you, Robbie, take the pile below. Can you flick through the cards and find the seven cards written down? When you've found them would you throw them onto the table, please?'

11 The audience still does not know what to expect, but it soon becomes apparent that Samuel and Robbie have thrown only six cards on the table and that the circled card is not there.

12 You say 'So a card is missing. Where is the nine of Diamonds? Please have another look through your piles. That was the card you circled Samuel. Well, it seems that my little experiment might be working.'

13 Select another member of the audience, say Rachel. 'What about the box, Rachel? It couldn't have got into there, could it? Perhaps you would pick it up and shake it.' Rachel shakes the box, which rattles. Say 'Did I hear a rattle, Rachel? There's something in there. Perhaps you would show us what it is?' Rachel opens the box and there is the nine of Diamonds.

Simple tricks

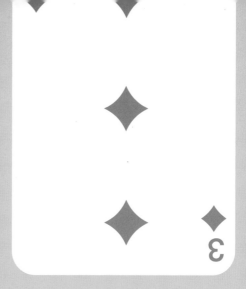

Tricks with prepared cards

In this section are a number of tricks which require packs of cards prepared in advance. Clearly you cannot perform a whole string of these together, because you would need a separate pack for each trick. But you could always have two or three prepared packs to hand so that you could introduce one of these baffling tricks from time to time.

Red or black

Skill level 2

You will need
One standard pack, prepared in advance.

The trick
The magician and the spectator have half of the pack each. They both deal their halves one at a time face down on the table into two piles separating by instinct the red cards from the black. At the end the cards are shown face up and, indeed, all the red cards and all the black cards are together.

How to do it

This is an exceedingly simple trick that you can perform with a prepared pack. It needs a pack in which all the red cards are together at the top of the pack and all the black at the bottom.

1 Take the pack from your pocket, look at it face up and divide it into two, red cards in one hand, black in the other. Obviously, you do not let the audience see this. Hand one half-pack to a member of the audience, say Grace, telling her to hold them face down and that she mustn't look at their faces.

2 Asking Grace to stand opposite or near you, tell her that you are both going to separate the red and black cards by instinct. Tell her that all she has to do is copy you.

3 You both start with your piles in your left hand, face down. You say to Grace 'It may surprise you, but if you have complete faith in yourself, you can sometimes sense whether a card is red or black. Just make your mind a blank, and deal your cards into two piles face down, the first pile to be those which instinct tells you are red, the second pile which instinct tells you are black. Look, I'll start, as I'm going to do the same with my cards. We'll see who does better.'

4 Begin dealing your cards irregularly into two piles, saying 'Red, red, black, red, black, black, black, red...', etc. Make sure that Grace does the same, but once she's started stop saying 'Red, black', just deal into two piles. Keep pace roughly with Grace, so that soon you each end with two piles in front of you, one supposedly red cards and one supposedly black.

5 Now you must pick up all four piles. Be careful not to say anything like 'This is your red pile and this is mine', or you'll likely have it pointed out that 'No, you're picking up my reds and your blacks', or something equally embarrassing.

6 Before saying anything, pick up the pile of Grace's cards nearest to your right with your right hand and swap it, face down, to your left hand. Pick up your right-hand pile and place it on top, followed by your left-hand pile. Then pick up the whole pile from your left hand smoothly and place it on top of the rest of Grace's cards, which are still on the table, then pick up the whole pack. Notice that you have all your original cards at one end of the pack, and all Grace's at the other. As you pick up the pack, say to the audience 'Now if Grace and I were both entirely right, we'd have all the red cards together and all the black cards together, but I suppose it would be too much to expect that. But let's see how close we were.'

7 Fan out the cards on the table, and just look, all the red cards are at one end of the pack and all the black at the other.

Flying cards

Skill level 2

You will need
Two identical packs, prepared in advance.

The trick
Two spectators are handed a pack each, which they cut. Each counts out 26 cards face down onto the table, putting one half-pack into their pockets while the other two half-packs are handed to two other spectators. These two spectators each choose a card from their packs that they remember and shuffle back into their half-packs. The magician then makes the cards they have chosen disappear, to be found in the other halves of the packs which all the time have been in the pockets of the spectators who held them first. The half-packs are joined together with their other halves and the packs are shown to be straightforward standard packs.

How to do it
This trick can baffle your audience completely. It requires two identically prepared packs.

1 To prepare the packs, arrange them both in exactly the same order. Then take 26 cards from the top of each pack and join them together. You now have a pack of 52 cards, but instead of all 52 cards being in the pack, there are 26 cards, each repeated twice. You also join up the bottom halves of the original two packs to make another pack. You put the two new packs back into their packets. Note that each pack contains 52 cards, but neither pack contains a card that is in the other pack.

2 Tell your audience that you need four volunteers, preferably two boys and two girls, to help with this trick and ask them to come and stand next to you so that all can see what is going on.

3 Hand the two specially prepared packs to the boys, say Andrew and George. Tell them they can cut the packs as often as they wish. This will not alter the order of the cards, but you must ensure they do not shuffle them. Now ask both of them to count out 26 cards face down onto the table and put the remainder of the pack into their pockets for safe keeping. Each half-pack on the table contains 26 different cards, and the two of them together make up a complete pack. But that's by the way.

4 Ask Andrew to take his half-pack from the table and give it to one of the girls, say to Jennifer, and George to hand his to the other, say Jessica.

5 Jennifer and Jessica now look at their cards and are asked to note and remember any one card. They can show it to others but mustn't tell you what the card is, and they must remember it. You then ask them to give their packs a good shuffle and take the two packs from them. You then tell them that what you are going to do is to make the cards they've chosen vanish from their packs and appear in the packs that Andrew and George have in their pockets.

6 While you're talking you have to perform the only piece of misdirection needed in this trick, because in a moment you are going to give Jessica and Jennifer their packs back, but you need to disguise that you are in fact giving Jennifer's pack to Jessica and vice versa.

7 So you do a little animated talking. You take Jennifer's and Jessica's packs from them one in each hand. Remind the spectators that Andrew and George counted 26 cards at random from their packs and passed them to Jennifer and Jessica. While doing this put Jessica's pack on top of Jennifer's crossways and hold both in your left hand. Tell them that Jennifer and Jessica each selected a card from their halves of the packs and remembered them. Transfer the two packs to your right hand. Hold them up to the audience and remind them that these packs are the other halves of the packs that George and Andrew have. Say to them 'Your halves of the packs have remained untouched in your pockets, haven't they? Perhaps you could put your hands round them to make sure nobody tampers with them.'

8 All this is so that everybody but you forgets which pack you took from Jessica and which from Jennifer. Hand back to Jessica and Jennifer their packs saying 'You two can now have your halves of the packs back.' You must be sure that each gets back the other's pack, or the trick doesn't work. Now ask Jennifer what her card was. Suppose she says 'Two of Spades.'

9 Now ask Andrew to take his cards from his pocket to see if the two of Spades has miraculously flown back there. It has!

10 You ask Jessica what her card was. Suppose she says 'The Queen of Diamonds.' Say to George 'Please take your cards from your pocket George and see if the Queen of Diamonds is among them.' It is!

11 Say to Jennifer and Jessica 'Well, unless the cards you picked really did fly to Andrew and George, there must be another two of Spades in your pack, Jennifer, and another Queen of Diamonds in your pack, Jessica. Let's see if you can find them.' They cannot! The cards have really jumped from the girls to the boys!

12 Now say 'They are quite ordinary packs. Will you Jennifer and Andrew hand your halves to Jade, and will you George and Jessica hand your halves to Gary. Now, Jade and Gary, will you count the cards to make sure there are 52 in each pack and that there appears to be one of each card in the pack? In other words that they are straightforward, complete and have not been tampered with?'

13 Jade and Gary confirm that this is so. Thank them and take the two packs back. 'Well, there you are, ladies and gentlemen – two completely ordinary packs. Except, of course, that the cards in them appear to have the ability of disappearing and reappearing elsewhere.'

Of course, the cards aren't so clever that they allow you to repeat the trick. You must pass on to another one.

Switching places

Skill level 3

You will need
A standard pack.

Special skills
The double lift.

The trick
A card whose identity is shown to the audience is laid face down on the table, followed by a second. The first card is returned to the pack. The magician, with a riffle of the pack, then makes the two cards change places.

How to do it

1 Ask a spectator to shuffle the pack thoroughly.

2 Take the pack back and square it up and at the same time establish the break below the top two cards which allows you to execute the double lift (see page 16). Tell the audience you wish to conduct a little experiment in the art of making cards change places. Say 'For example, let's take the top card of the pack, which happens to be...' Double-lift the top two cards from the pack, look at the exposed card and say its name, '...the nine of Clubs.'

3 Show the card to the audience, and replace the two cards on the top of the pack.

4 Continue 'What we'll do, is place the nine of Clubs here on the table.' Place the top card of the pack, which of course is *not* the nine of Clubs, on the table face down. Say 'The next thing to do is to take the second card from the pack.' While you are saying this, prepare for another double lift, which you now make.

5 The top card of the pack is now, as you know, the nine of Clubs. But when you double-lift the top two cards, you show the audience the next card – let's say it's the ten of Diamonds. Returning the double lift to the pack, you say 'We'll put the ten of Diamonds on the table here next to the nine of Clubs.' Taking the top card, which is the nine of Clubs, place it at least six inches to the right of the first card, so there can be no confusion as to which card is which.

Tricks with prepared cards

57

6 Say 'Now I'll pick up the nine of Clubs and return it to the top of the pack.' Pick up the first card and do this. Say to the audience 'The situation now is that on top of the pack we have the nine of Clubs and on the table we have the ten of Diamonds. What I'm going to attempt is to make them change places.'

7 With the pack in your left hand, riffle the cards with your right. While saying something like 'I hope that's enough to do the trick – it isn't easy, you know', you get a break beneath the top two cards to execute your third double lift.

8 Double-lift the top two cards and show them to the audience, saying 'If I'm successful, this should be the ten of Diamonds.' When the audience have seen that it is, turn it to look at it yourself, and feign pleasure and relief when you discover that it is, indeed, the ten of Diamonds. Place the double lift back on the pack, saying 'And, of course, if the cards really *did* change places, this one on the table should be the nine of Clubs.' Lift it up and show it to the audience to reveal that it is.

TIP

During this trick, you perform three double lifts. This is not a difficult sleight – you should master it easily with practice – but it is one in which you have to establish a break between the top two cards and the remainder with your left little finger. You must do this before you actually say 'Let's take the top card of the pack...' because at that time your audience will look at your hand taking the 'top' card and it will be too late to establish the finger-break. Develop the habit of holding the pack in your left hand and squaring it up with your right while you are talking to the audience. In this way, you can establish the break well in advance, and be executing the double lift almost before you tell the audience that you are going to show them the top card.

The upturned card

Skill level 2

You will need
An arranged pack.

Special skills
False shuffle.

The trick
From a shuffled pack, a spectator picks a card, and replaces it on top of the pack, which is again shuffled and cut. The magician cuts the pack until he finds an upturned four of Diamonds, which he throws on the table. The spectator protests that this is not his card. The magician says the four merely tells him to count off four cards, which he does, laying them in a line on the table. He turns up the fifth card, which is that chosen by the spectator. He then turns over the four cards on the table, which turn out to be the four Aces.

How to do it
You begin this trick with a pack arranged as follows: at the bottom are the four Aces, and next to them is the four of Diamonds *face up*.

1 Execute a couple of false shuffles, keeping the group of five cards together at the bottom of the pack (see false shuffle 7, page 14).

2 Now fan out the cards and ask a member of the audience, say Max, to pick one. When fanning the cards keep the lower cards unfanned in your left hand to make sure that he does not choose a card from among the bottom five and that he can't see the upturned four of Diamonds.

3 When Max has taken his card ask him to show it to the others and remember it. Suppose it is the King of Spades. Close the cards and ask Max to put the card back on top of the pack, without letting you see it. Complete a cut of the cards to bring Max's card below the group of Aces, with the whole group of significant cards (now numbering six) together near the middle of the pack.

The four aces

4
♦

The arrangement of
the pack before the
start of the trick.

4 Now tell Max 'I am about to do
something really extraordinary: in
fact, I am going to find your card by
making a card turn over and appear in
the pack face up.'

5 Slowly fan through the cards until
you reach the four of Diamonds,
which is face up. Place on the table the
part of the pack above the four, then lay
down the four of Diamonds and say
'There you are, the four of Diamonds.'
   Look satisfied until Max says 'No it
isn't, you've got it wrong.'

6 Smile and say 'No, I haven't. I
didn't say *this* was your card, did I?
The four of Diamonds just tells me to
count out four cards.' Count out the next
four cards in a line, face down, and turn
the fifth one face up. 'What I'm saying is
that *this* is your card.' Max has to admit
it is.

7 Say 'Well, I knew it had to be the
King of Spades.' As an
afterthought, say 'After all, it couldn't be
one of these, could it?' and turn over the
four face-down cards, which are shown
to be the four Aces.

Tricks with prepared cards

Clocking on

Skill level 3

You will need
A prepared pack, pen and paper, envelope (plus a marked card, scissors and sticky tape for the alternative double-kick version).

Special skills
False shuffle.

The trick
In this trick a magician writes a prediction on a piece of paper and places it in an envelope. Then he lays down a shuffled pack on the table and, turning his back, asks a person from the audience to take any number of cards between one and twelve from the top. Then the magician deals out 12 cards from the top of the pack and forms a clockface with them, with the 12 cards representing the numbers on the dial. The magician then asks the helper the number of cards in the envelope and to turn over the card representing that number on the clock face. Then he asks her to open the envelope and look at his prediction. It will predict the card that she has turned over.

How to do it
You need a sheet of paper, pen, an envelope and a prepared pack for this trick. Or, at least, you need to know the identity of the thirteenth card down from the top of a face-down pack. You could try looking at the cards in a pack earlier, but the trick will be more effective if you do it after another one so that the audience are less likely to suspect that you have prepared the pack (see Following on from another trick, page 64). Let us assume that the thirteenth card down is the King of Diamonds.

1 Tell the audience that the next trick you will do involves an amazing prediction, which you are going to write on a piece of paper and pass to a volunteer in the audience for safe keeping.

2 Without letting the audience see it, write on a sheet of paper 'I predict that you will select the King of Diamonds.' Fold the sheet of paper and put it in the envelope. Do not seal the envelope yet, but lay it on the table in front of you. Tell the audience you will give the pack a quick shuffle, and perform false shuffle 1 (page 11), retaining the vital 13 cards on the top of the pack.

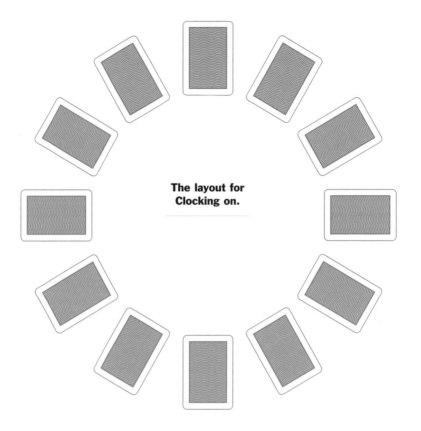

**The layout for
Clocking on.**

3 Place the pack on the table and ask for a volunteer – let's say Imogen. Tell her you are going to turn your back while she takes any number of cards between one and twelve from the top of the pack. Tell her to do it quietly because you mustn't know how many she's taken, but she must remember this number. When she's done this, tell her you are going to turn round so she must be careful not to let you see how many cards she has in her hand.

4 Then ask her to take the envelope with the prediction in it, place her cards in the envelope alongside the prediction and seal it.

5 Now turn round and take up the rest of the pack, saying 'We are going to create a clockface for this little operation so I shall need 12 cards, one for each number on the clock.' Count out 12 cards face down onto the table from the pack, counting aloud from 1 to 12 as you go. Put the rest of the pack aside and take up the 12 cards.

6 Beginning at one o'clock lay out the 12 cards clock-face style, saying as you lay each one down 'One o'clock, two o'clock, three o'clock...' up to twelve o'clock. The layout will be as in the illustration above.

7 Now say to Imogen 'If you remember, Imogen, the cards were shuffled, you took off as many as you liked without me knowing how many. Now tell me how many cards you put in the envelope.'

8 Suppose Imogen says 'Five.' Say to her 'OK, will you please turn over the card corresponding to five o'clock on the clock face.' Imogen does so, and the card proves to be the King of Diamonds.

9 Say 'Imogen, you could have chosen any number of cards, but by choosing five, you have selected the King of Diamonds. Now will you please open the envelope and read out my prediction?'

10 Imogen does so, and reads out 'I predict you will select the King of Diamonds.'

Explanation

However many cards Imogen puts in the envelope, the King of Diamonds, which was originally the thirteenth card in the pack, will be the card corresponding to that number on the clockface. When Imogen put the top five cards into the envelope, the King of Diamonds became the eighth card in the pack. When the top 12 cards were dealt face down to the table, the King of Diamonds became the fifth from the top, and therefore went into the five o'clock position. Had Imogen taken six cards, the King of Diamonds would have become the

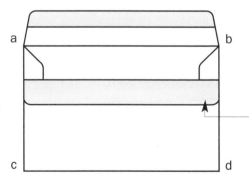

a

b

Folded sticky tape to
stick sheet ABCD on
inside of envelope

Gum on underside of flap

c

d

Cut the front of another envelope, write on it the prediction, and with sticky tape stick it inside the envelope to make a false compartment.

You will choose the two of clubs

FOLLOWING ON FROM ANOTHER TRICK

You could do this trick after, say, An improved memory trick (see page 26), which ends with 21 face-up cards scattered on the table. After holding up the spectator's chosen card and showing it to the audience, pick up a group of seven more cards, without making it obvious that you're picking up a particular number – it will not be difficult – and transfer the eight you now hold to your left hand, face down. As if you are taking too long, sweep the remaining 13 cards on the table into a rough, face-up pile and pick them up with your right hand. Memorize the top card and add them face down onto the pile in your left hand. Add the pile to the rest of the pack, and now you know the identity of the thirteenth card from the top.

seventh card in the pack and therefore the sixth card dealt to the table, in the six o'clock position, and so on. The King will always correspond on the clockface to the number of cards in the envelope.

An alternative double-kick version

In the alternative version you do not ask how many cards are in the envelope, but are guided, Ouija-board fashion, to the number on the clock that represents the number of cards in the envelope. While the audience is thinking about that piece of magic you reveal a prediction you placed in the envelope earlier that identified the card to which you were guided. You must decide for yourself whether you prefer this to the simpler version.

1 If you wish to amaze your audience with the extra revelation on this trick, you must prepare the pack in advance by marking the thirteenth card. You need only the tiniest mark on the back of the card to be able to recognize it when you have the whole back in view. If there is a space in the design on the pack, just put a tiny pencil mark in it, using a coloured pencil of the same colour as the back of the card. Nobody else will notice it. At worst, make a tiny pencil mark at a point on the white margin around the pattern. Let's assume you mark the two of Clubs.

2 With this knowledge, the routine of the trick changes. You prepare your prediction in advance. Take an identical envelope to the one you are going to use (in this case it's best to use self-sealing envelopes with gum on two flaps that require no licking) and cut off the whole of the front. Write on one side 'You will choose the two of Clubs.' Then with a strip of sticky tape hinge this on the inside of the envelope, so that the prediction is invisible (see page 63). The effect is that the envelope has a false 'compartment' containing the prediction. Have the scissors to hand when you perform this version of the trick.

3 Ask a member of the audience, let's say Imogen as before, to remove between one and twelve cards from the pack. When this is done, open the envelope for her, holding it with the flap open, and flap side down, so that she can slip in her chosen number of cards without you seeing how many and, just as important, without her noticing that the envelope has been tampered with. Then push up the lower flap for her and while you hold the bottom of the envelope ask her to seal it.

4 When you deal out the 12 cards and make the clock face, you will spot immediately the marked card and know from its position how many cards were put into the envelope.

5 Now place another card face down in the centre of the clockface. Say to Imogen 'Concentrate on the number of cards you put into the envelope for a minute and I will put my fingers on this card and let your thoughts direct me to a number on the clockface.' Pretend to go into a semi-trance, and move the card erratically round a little before a final decisive push moves it towards the marked card. Let's assume it is at eight o'clock. Toss the card you've been moving to one side and say to Imogen 'The strength of your thoughts has pushed me towards eight o'clock, so I

predict the number of cards in the envelope is eight. Is that correct?'

6 Imogen will confirm that this was so. Ask her to take the cards from the envelope and hand them to you. The audience will assume that this is the end of the trick. But say to Imogen 'Out of interest, would you please turn over the card you picked out at eight o'clock? She will do so. You say 'Ah – the two of Clubs.' Collect up all the other cards on the table, leaving the two of Clubs there. Say 'Now that's a very interesting card, the two of Clubs. I'll explain why. You then produce your pair of scissors.

7 Say to Imogen 'Would you mind cutting a thin strip from the bottom of the envelope. Now, if you slit up the sides of the envelope, you will find that there's an inner compartment, which contains a message. Would you please read it out?'

8 Imogen reads 'You will choose the two of Clubs.' Say 'There, I told you there was something special about the two of Clubs.'

A neat trick with a double kick.

Queen for the day

Skill level 3

You will need
A prepared pack.

Special skill
False shuffle.

The trick
A spectator makes four piles from a shuffled pack. She then moves cards from top to bottom of each pile and from each pile to the other piles. When finally she is asked to turn over the top cards of each pile they are revealed to be the four Queens.

How to do it
For this trick, the pack has to be prepared in advance, so that the four Queens are the top four cards when the pack is face down.

1 I like to do this trick by asking a girl in the audience to help. Suppose Katie volunteers to help. You tell her you'll just give the pack a quick shuffle first and you perform the false overhand shuffle 1 (see page 11), retaining the four Queens on top of the pack. This disguises the fact that you're using a prepared pack.

2 Lay the pack on the table in front of Katie and tell her you want the pack cut into a row of four more or less equal piles. Ask her to pick up the pack, drop off about a quarter into one pile, a similar amount into a second pile next to it, then a third pile, so that the rest of the pack makes a fourth pile at the end of the row. If you ask her to do it like this you will end up with the four Queens on top of the fourth pile. (If you ask her to make four piles in her own way, you

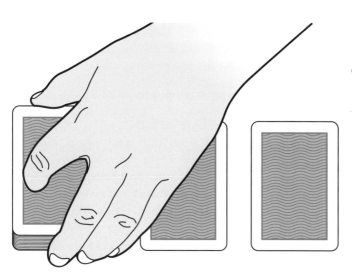

The spectator making the third of a line of four piles by dropping off about a quarter of the pack each time.

might find the four Queens will be on top of the second pile, say, which will make the next part of the trick awkward and clumsy.)

3 Pointing to the first pile, you now say to Katie 'Pick up pile 1, and without looking at them transfer the top three cards to the bottom of the pile. Good. Now deal one card from the top, face down, onto each of the other three piles.' When she has done this, ask her to replace her pile where it was on the table. Then, again pointing so there are no mistakes, ask her to pick up pile 2, and repeating the instructions, get her to do the same procedure with pile 2 as she did with pile 1. Repeat the move with piles 3 and 4.

4 Now say to Katie 'Well, Katie, you cut the cards into four piles yourself and then moved the cards from top to bottom and from one pile to the other, so would you agree it would be impossible to know which cards are at the top of each pile?'

5 Unless she is a particularly argumentative type, Katie will agree with you. You then say 'Well the strange thing about this exercise is that often, if the person who operated the cards has a strong personality, the cards at the top of the piles will reflect this in some way. So unless you're unwilling to reveal what the cards say about you would you like to turn over the four top cards?'

6 Katie, to general amazement, will turn over the four Queens. Say 'Well, Katie, congratulations, the cards seem to be saying that you're a Queen.'

Tricks with prepared cards

The identical card

Skill level 3

You will need
A standard pack.

Special skills
Roly-poly pass, false shuffle.

The trick
A spectator shuffles, picks a card from a fan and replaces it in the centre of the pack. The pack is shuffled and split into two. The spectator chooses which half he wants, the magician takes the other. The magician and the spectator both lay four cards from their packs face down to the table. The spectator makes a series of choices which leave one card of the eight on the table. It turns out to be the chosen card.

How to do it
This is an excellent use of what is known as the 'conjuror's choice', where the spectator thinks he is choosing from alternative cards or piles but in reality is having the choice forced on him by the magician.

1 Give a volunteer, who we'll call Simon, the pack to shuffle. Take it back, fan it out and ask him to select a card, look at it and remember it. Let's assume this is the ten of Spades. While he is doing this, square up the cards in your left and right hands, and ask him to place his card on the pile in your left hand.

2 Execute the roly-poly pass (see page 22) with the two halves of the pack and go straight into false shuffle 1 (see page 11) which will keep the ten of Spades on top of the pack. Place the pack on the table and ask Simon to cut it into two halves.

3 Ask him to take which half he wants while you take the other. It doesn't matter which half Simon chooses, but you must remember which of you has the half-pack that is topped by the ten of Spades. Let us suppose he has it.

4 Say 'Now, Simon, what we have to do is find your chosen card. First, we must both lay a row of four cards face down on the table in front of us.' Do this. Ask for the cards Simon is still holding, add them to yours and discard them all, face down, on the side.

5 Each of you now has a row of four cards in front of you. The first card in Simon's row is the ten of Spades. Say to him 'Would you please indicate one of these rows, Simon?'

6 If he indicates or says 'Yours', you say 'OK, we need only one row' and pick it up and add it to the other discarded cards. If he indicates his, say 'OK' and pick up and discard your four cards. This is the 'conjuror's choice'. Whichever he picks, his row of four cards remains on the table, with the ten of Spades at the end.

7 Now ask Simon to choose two of the cards on the table, by putting a finger on both. Whichever pair he points to, ask him if he's sure, and whether he'd like to change his mind. Whether he does or not, he'll end by pointing to two cards. Emphasize that this is his final choice – he cannot change now. If his choice includes the ten of Spades pick up the other two and say 'Fine. It's a free world, that's your choice.' Add the two cards to the discards.

8 If Simon keeps his fingers on the two cards, say to him 'We're down to two cards. All you have to do now is lift your finger off one, and we'll have our final card, which we'll use to discover your original chosen card which is presumably in the pack over there.' Indicate the discard pile. Putting it like this to Simon encourages him to think about what might be coming next, rather than to think about his choice, which could lead to him suspecting that the final card is being forced upon him. Of course, if Simon lifts his finger off the ten of Spades you pick up the other, saying, 'This is the final discard then', and discard it.

9 If, on the other hand, Simon places his fingers on two cards that do *not* include the ten of Spades, you must take those two cards from under his fingers and say 'OK. These then are the next two discards, leaving us with just two cards. We need only one to help us find your original chosen card, which is presumably hiding in the pack over there, so perhaps for the last time you'd finger a card.' If he puts his finger on the ten of Spades, pick up and discard the other. If his finger goes to the other card, pick it up, saying 'This then is the final discard.'

You can see that whatever Simon does at each of his three choices, you can convincingly leave his original chosen card, the ten of Spades, as the final card on the table.

10 You can now say 'Right. We now have a card on the table chosen entirely by you from a pack which you shuffled and cut yourself, and I think this card will be the key to discovering the whereabouts of the card you picked from the pack in the first place. So what was that card?' While saying this, pick up the pack of discarded cards as if you are about somehow to discover Simon's card in it.

11 Simon names the card as the ten of Spades. Say 'So what card have you chosen to try to find it? Please turn it over.' The card turns out to be the ten of Spades. Pretend dismay. Say 'Well, you've just spoilt the whole trick, Simon. Do you always have to pick out the ten of Spades? I won't ask you to pick a card again.'

Queen and Jack swap

Skill level 4

You will need
An arranged pack, which includes an extra Queen of Diamonds from an identical pack.

Special skills
False shuffle, double lift, palming.

The trick
A girl spectator is handed the top card of a shuffled pack to hold. This card, a Jack, represents her. Another spectator, a boy, is handed the second card in the pack, which turns out to be a Queen, to represent him. The two spectators hold their cards face down between their hands. The magician makes the cards change places, so that the boy is more suitably represented by the Jack, and the girl by the Queen.

How to do it
This trick requires a doctored pack, a false shuffle, a double lift and a palming, so it is an excellent trick for you to do when you are confident with these techniques.

1 You need a Queen of Diamonds from an identical pack to the one you are going to use. Before performing the trick you arrange that the top three cards are the Queen of Diamonds, Jack of Clubs, and the other Queen of Diamonds. Ask a boy and girl from the audience to help you. Let's call them Aaron and Lucy. Say to the audience 'To show there's nothing dodgy going on, we'll give the pack a quick shuffle.'

2 Perform the false shuffle (see page 11) to retain the Queen, Jack, Queen sequence at the top of the pack.

The order of the cards at the top of the pack to begin, with the Jack of Clubs between the two Queens of Diamonds.

3 Establish a break with your little finger below the top two cards. Say 'What I will do first is to ask Lucy to represent the card on top of the pack.' Execute a double lift, turning the 'card' over and laying it on the pack face up to show to Lucy and the audience that it is the Jack of Clubs. Say 'It's the Jack of Clubs.' Return the 'card' face down to the top of the pack.

4 Say to Lucy 'Now you Lucy, for the purpose of this operation, represent the Jack of Clubs. In fact I want you to look after it for me for a minute or two. Please hold out your left hand.' Place the top card of the pack (which in fact is the Queen of Diamonds) face down on Lucy's hand. Say 'Now please place your right hand over the Jack of Clubs and hold it secure while I deal with Aaron.'

5 Give the cards another false shuffle, and under cover of this establish a break below the two top cards again.

6 Turn to Aaron and say 'Now Aaron, we'll see what card you represent.' Say to Aaron 'How strange, you are the Queen of Diamonds. But don't be offended' (while saying this turn the 'card' face down again on top of the pack and square it up) 'because this suits what I want to do very nicely. Hold out your hand and you hold the Queen of Diamonds for me for the moment.' Place the 'Queen of Diamonds' (which is in fact the Jack of Clubs) face down in Aaron's hand and ask him to cover it up with his other hand.

7 Now say 'It's very strange, but the fact that Lucy got the Jack of Clubs and Aaron the Queen of Diamonds was actually a very good piece of luck for me, for the point of this little exercise is for me to swap the cards around. Now you may think that this is impossible, but it's not. Now, Lucy, you represent the Jack of Clubs, right?' (Lucy agrees.) 'Now I'm sure you'd rather be the Queen of Diamonds, wouldn't you?' (Lucy agrees again.) 'Well, look at your card and see who you represent.'

8 Lucy turns over her card. It is the Queen of Diamonds! Turn to Aaron and say 'Now, Aaron, I bet you're glad that you don't have to be a Queen for the night.' (Aaron agrees.) 'Well, I said I would swap the two around, and if you'll kindly look at your card, I think you'll find that I did.' Aaron looks at his card and finds it's the Jack of Clubs.

9 Take the cards from Lucy and Aaron and return them to the pack, saying 'Well, I knew I could do it, but it was a very nice coincidence that we should get the Queen and the Jack turned up like that. I couldn't have asked for more.'

10 You will have spotted that if you did everything as described, you will now have a pack of cards containing two Queens of Diamonds, which is not good, as you'll want to carry on using the pack for more tricks.

11 Also, somebody might ask to see the pack, and it's better to let them and prove that the pack was a regular one. So after giving Aaron his card to hold, and while explaining how lucky you were about the two cards used being the Queen and Jack, continue to square up the cards in your hands. When Lucy reveals her card, everybody will look at her, and you can casually palm the top card of the pack, which is, of course, the spare Queen of Diamonds. Drop your hand to your side, then when Aaron reveals his card, and becomes the centre of attention, casually put your right hand in your pocket and dispose of the palmed card. When you take back Aaron's and Lucy's cards, you will have a regular 52-card pack in your hands, which anybody can examine (though do not suggest it, appear to agree to an inspection reluctantly if asked). In any case, if you've performed well, you will have a baffled and appreciative audience before you.

Tricks with prepared cards

73

Memorizing the telephone book

Skill level 4

You will need
A prepared pack, a telephone directory, pencil and paper.

Special skills
A false shuffle, double-turnover force and memorizing a telephone book entry.

The trick
Spectators cut a shuffled pack and the first four cards below the cut are handed to four other spectators. The four ranks of the cards are written down to represent a three-digit number and a separate number. The telephone directory is fetched and the page denoted by the three-digit number is turned to. The entry denoted by the odd number is found, and the magician reads out the name, address and telephone number of the entry thus chosen.

How to do it

1 Tell your audience that you are going to perform a prodigious feat of memory. Tell them that these days so many people have forgotten the knack of remembering telephone numbers, because they just enter them in their telephones' memories, but you have developed your memory and will prove just what is possible.

2 Produce a pack of cards, which is prepared to the extent that you know the top four cards. Let us say that they are the two of Diamonds, Ace of Clubs, eight of Hearts and nine of Spades.

3 Say 'I'll give the cards a good shuffle.' Execute a few false shuffles, keeping the top four cards intact at the top. Now you must force these four cards on to members of the audience. I suggest you use the double-turnover force (see page 21).

4 When two volunteers have each cut and turned over part of the pack, and you get down to the first face-down card, you ask one of your audience, say Daniel, to take it and look after it. As you know, it will be the two of Diamonds. Then ask Hermione to take the next card, which of course is the Ace of Clubs. Tell Hermione to hold on to it for a minute, and ask Megan to take the next card. Megan looks after the eight of Hearts and you ask David to take the next card – the nine of Spades.

5 Now take the pencil and paper and say 'We've got four cards taken completely at random from a shuffled pack. Now Daniel, what is yours?' Daniel tells you and you say 'A two. I'll write down two.' You ask Hermione and Megan in turn and add their numbers and say 'We've now got 218.' (An Ace, of course, counts as one.) 'So let's take 218 as a page number. Now what is your card, David?' David says nine of Spades. You say 'Right. We'll take that as the ninth entry on the page. So we have page 218, entry 9, numbers which you'll agree I couldn't possibly have predicted. Now, Emily, would you go and fetch that telephone directory over there, please? Thank you. Now if you open it at page 218 and look down to the ninth

entry on that page, I will try to tell you the telephone number.'

6 Make a great show of concentrating hard, fingers pressed against temples and all the rest of it. Then say 'Let's see. I think this entry is for somebody called W.P. Thomas, who lives at 27 Georgian Close, Wexton. Have I got the right entry?' Emily says you have. Say 'Well, now is the difficult part – remembering his number. I'm pretty sure Mr Thomas's number is 838 (thinking hard) and I reckon 1971. Am I right?'

7 Emily confirms you are correct, which of course is no surprise to you, as you've carefully remembered this complete line from the telephone directory in advance.

Your audience will be amazed as you ask Emily to put the directory back and you collect up the cards from your other kind assistants.

Tricks with prepared cards

Amazing memory feat

Skill level 4

You will need
A prepared pack of cards.

The trick
The magician shows the audience a well-mixed pack, shuffles the cards, places them on the table and cuts them, completing the cut. A member of the audience is asked to complete a cut, and other members of the audience are invited to cut should they wish to. Then a spectator takes a number of cards from the top – if the audience does not exceed ten say, one for each member of the audience (if the audience is more than ten then limit the number to ten). The spectator shuffles the ten cards and distributes them among members of the audience. The magician takes the pack back and claims that by fanning through the cards once, he will be able to name most of the missing ones. He fans slowly through the cards, places the pack on the table and recites the names of all the missing cards.

How to do it
This trick relies upon the whole pack being arranged in order. The cards are arranged so that without analysing the pack closely nobody would think the cards were in anything but random order. However, they are cleverly arranged in a manner that makes it easy for you to remember the sequence. It is, reading from top left downwards and so on:

8C	8H	8S	8D
KH	KS	KD	KC
3S	3D	3C	3H
10D	10C	10H	10S
2C	2H	2S	2D
7H	7S	7D	7C
9S	9D	9C	9H
5D	5C	5H	5S
QC	QH	QS	QD
4H	4S	4D	4C
AS	AD	AC	AH
6D	6C	6H	6S
JC	JH	JS	JD

The face-up pack therefore runs from the eight of Clubs through the King of Hearts and so on to the Jack of Diamonds at the bottom.

You remember by using this following ten-word rhyming couplet and a single word.

Eight Kings threatened to save
Ninety-five ladies for one sick Knave

This translates as:

Eight, King, three, ten, two, seven
Nine, five, Queen, four, one, six, Jack
(Knave)

You can remember the order of the suits by remembering the single word CHaSeD, which gives you Clubs, Hearts, Spades, Diamonds.

1 Take the prepared pack and fan it out before the audience, saying 'As you can see we have an ordinary, well-mixed pack.' Pretend to shuffle it by making, in effect, a series of cuts in your hand. With the pack face down in your left hand, take a pile from the bottom and take it over to the top, as in the ordinary shuffle. Do this three or four times. Do not say you're shuffling the cards, or somebody might tell you that you are not. Just let those who want to believe you are shuffling that you are. You are, of course, not keeping the pack exactly the same, in that the top card

will not remain the eight of Clubs but the *order* of the cards will not be affected.

2 Put the cards on the table and complete a straightforward cut. Ask a spectator to complete a cut, and then another. Say 'Would anybody else like to cut?' If so, let them. Then choose one of the audience, let's call her Sophie, and ask her to make a final cut and then to take ten cards (or however many is appropriate) from the top and return the rest of the pack to the table. Ask Sophie to shuffle the ten cards thoroughly and share them among ten members of the audience.

3 Say 'I am now going to perform a feat of concentration and memory. By looking through the remaining cards of the pack once and once only, I am going to try to recognize and call out the ten cards that are shared among you. I know it sounds impossible and I might not get them all, but if I get, say, eight, I'm sure you'll agree it would be a fantastic effort. Agreed?'

4 Pick up the pack and make a show of concentrating as hard as you can on the cards as you fan through them. This is a pure act, because all you need to do is look at the bottom card. But you must pretend to look at every card. Make as big a fan as you can in your hand, so that you appear to be looking at as many as you can at a time.

5 Finally, fold up the fan and place the cards face down on the table. Let us say the bottom card was the five of Clubs.

6 Now you can, of course, reel off the ten cards quite quickly, but that would be boring and unconvincing. As the bottom card is a five, the next card in the sequence as you remember it from the rhyme is a Queen, which is useful. You know, in fact, that it is the Queen of Hearts, as Hearts follows Clubs. So you begin straight away by saying 'One of the cards is the Queen of Hearts. Missing picture cards are easy enough to spot, especially the Queen of Hearts, who made the tarts. Does somebody have the Queen of Hearts? Would you place it face up on the table, please? Thank you. Now another card I noticed quickly was the four of Spades. Anybody have that? Good. Aces are distinctive cards and I noticed only one of those was missing, the Ace of Diamonds. If anybody's got that, would they lay it down please? Thanks. OK so far. Now it gets harder. I know the six of Clubs was missing – oh, and of course the Jack of Hearts, who stole the tarts, he's missing. How many have I got so far? Five? Now it gets harder. The eight

of Spades I think wasn't there... oh, the King of Diamonds of course, I'd forgotten him.'

7 Now start to hesitate and think of the cards a little slower. You can see you have seven cards on the table, so there are only three to go.

8 Suddenly continue 'The three of Clubs, I'm pretty sure was missing, right, and as I try to visualize what cards are in the pack, I don't recall seeing the ten of Hearts. Has anybody got that one?' Think a bit more, saying 'Well this last one is a bit of a problem. It must be a small one, and I'm pretty sure it's black. I think I'll go for the two of Spades.'

9 As the two of Spades is laid on the table, look suddenly relaxed as if you've come out of a trance, and say 'Well, I didn't expect to get all right. Ten is about my limit.' As you collect up the cards, continue 'I have seen a magician who had 49 cards shared out among the audience and he managed to name the lot. Absolutely stunning performance, it was.' Let this sink in. It is of course a joke, as any magician who is given three cards ought to be able to name the other 49 from memory. But if the audience doesn't see it, let it pass...

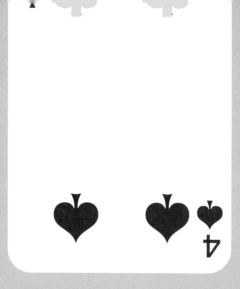

More advanced magic

This section contains tricks which require the use of one or more of the special skills from the Sleights and shuffles chapter (see page 8). These are tricks which, when performed well, will give you the aura of a real magician. Practise them all before you decide to impress your audience with them.

A big hit

Skill level 2

You will need
A standard pack.

Special skills
The peek, the glide.

The trick
A spectator chooses a card from a fanned-out, face-down pack, remembers it and places the card back on top of the pack, which she cuts to return the card to the centre. The magician says he will find the card. He picks up about a third of the pack, fans through and cannot find it. He takes up half of the remaining pack, fans through and still cannot find the card. Nor does the remainder of the pack reveal the card. Apologizing, the magician says he will try another method. Dividing the pack in two, he asks the spectator to choose which half to use. Taking it up, the magician holds it in his left hand and smacks the pack with his right. All the cards fall to the floor except one, which turns out to be the chosen card.

How to do it
This is my version of a very old trick, which is not performed much these days but worth doing for its startling ending.

1 Ask an onlooker, say Alice, to shuffle the pack and hand it back to you. Try to get a peek at the bottom card as she finishes shuffling – if you can't, take a peek as you take back the cards. Fan them out face down and ask Alice to take one from anywhere, to look at it and remember it. As she is doing this square up the pack and place it on the table. Tell Alice to add her card to the top of the pack. Place your fingers lightly on the card on the top of the pack, telling Alice you are getting a feel of her card. Ask her to cut the cards so that her card is buried in the middle of the pack.

2 Tell Alice that from the feel you have a pretty good idea of what her card is and that you are now going to identify it. Pick up just under a third of the pack and fan through it face up, as if you are looking for a particular card. Say 'I don't think it's in this pile', and set the pile down on the table. Take up slightly more than half of the remaining pile and do the same.

3 If Alice's card was cut to near the middle of the pack, it will probably be in this pile. You will identify it because it will be above, i.e. one to the right of, the card you took a peek at

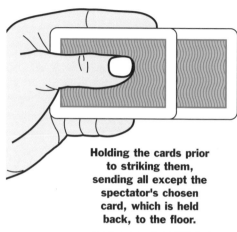

Making a double fan. The second row is held between the index and middle fingers. The fan is separated at the Ace of Hearts (the spectator's card) and the five of Spades (the marker card).

Holding the cards prior to striking them, sending all except the spectator's chosen card, which is held back, to the floor.

originally. When you come to it, you must contrive to get it to the left-hand side of the fan. The best way is as follows. When you come to Alice's card, make a break in the fan, as if you are attempting to make a fan of too many cards. Begin making a second fan in front of the first (see above). When you have the two fans spread, look puzzled and say 'Well, I would have thought it was among these cards, but I'm not sure now. Let's have a look at the rest.'

4 Fold the two fans together, and place the pile face down on the pile you've already looked at. You've now managed to get Alice's card on top of the face-down pile. Take up the remainder of the cards you haven't yet scrutinized, saying 'Well, Alice's card must be in here.'

5 Fan through and say with disappointment 'Well, nothing here gives me any vibes, either. It's disappointing, because I rarely fail with this exercise.' As you are talking, close up the fan, hold the cards face down in your left hand and pick up the pile from the table. Add it to the pile in your left hand, and you now have the whole pack face down with Alice's card on top.

6 Saying 'Well, one mustn't despair. I'm going to try another method', place the pack on the table and divide it into two halves by cutting it. Say to Alice 'You choose one of these piles.'

7 If Alice chooses the pile with her card on top, say 'Fine', and take it up in your hand. If she chooses the other, say 'OK, I'll have this one then', taking up the pile she didn't choose. In either case, you have half of the pack in your hand with Alice's card on top. This way of making the spectator choose but still getting the pile you want is known as 'the conjuror's choice'.

8 Take the cards in your left hand, and hold them at right angles to the floor, with the backs towards you. Pull the top card back with your thumb as if for the glide (see page 83). Make sure the audience are unaware of the glide. They shouldn't be suspicious, as they do not know what you are going to do.

9 Say 'Desperate situations require desperate remedies. I am now going to resort to brute force and ignorance. Ready?' As you finish speaking, bring your right hand down, little finger first in a chopping movement, on the protruding part of the pack you are holding. All the cards will shoot to the floor, except Alice's card, which will automatically be grasped between fingers and thumb. Practise this and you will see that it works. It is easiest if your left thumb is moistened before you hit into the cards, but I feel that licking your thumb before performing the trick detracts from it too much. The trick will work without, and a little practice will show you how best to position your thumb, how tightly to hold the cards and how hard to hit them.

OBSERVATIONS

You can make this trick more spectacular by hitting the cards from below, showering them into the air, but you will then probably need to collect them from all over the place. Whether you choose to hit up or down, you have to pick up the cards from the floor. It is therefore an opportunity to arrange the order slightly to suit perhaps a following trick, for example you could easily arrange the pack for the trick called Clocking on (see page 61). The audience could hardly suspect a prepared pack when you've just picked most of them up from the floor.

10 When the cards have all scattered, turn your left hand palm upwards, withdrawing your thumb as you do so and without looking at the card offer it face down to Alice, saying 'Your card, I believe?'

Two for the price of one

Skill level 3

You will need
A standard pack.

Special skills
Peeking, false shuffle.

The trick
A member of the audience deals 16 cards as directed and is left with one card which she memorizes and places back on the pack. Another spectator repeats the exercise and remembers the card he picked. Both shuffle the 16 cards. The magician then fans out the 16 cards and lays two of his choice on the table. The two members announce their cards and the magician turns over the two cards, which are proved to tally.

How to do it

1 Pick up the pack, taking a peek (see page 18) at the bottom card. Let's say it's the Queen of Hearts. Perform false shuffles (see page 11) to bring it to the top. Pass the pack to a spectator, say Claire, and ask her to deal 16 cards face down to the table. The bottom card of the 16 will be the Queen of Hearts.

2 Pick them up and say you'd just like to check there are 16, and deal them to the table again, counting one to sixteen as you go. The top card is now the Queen of Hearts again. Pick up the cards and square them up on the table, peeking at the new bottom card. Let's say it's the three of Clubs. You now know both the top and bottom cards.

3 Hand the cards to Jack, and ask him to deal them to the table face down as follows: the top card to the table, the next to the bottom of the pile, the next to the table, the next to the bottom of the pile, and so on until only one card is left in his hand. Ask him to look at it, remember it, and place it face down on top of the pile. It will be the three of Clubs unless he has misdealt. You must watch closely for misdeals.

4 When Jack has finished, push the cards to Claire (squaring them up if necessary) and ask her to do the same as Jack. She will find, if she follows instructions properly, that her last card is the Queen of Hearts. Ask her to remember it carefully and place it on the pile. Ask Claire now to give the pile a good shuffle, then to pass it to Jack for him to shuffle. Then take the pile back and fan it out so that you can see the cards. Pick out the three of Clubs and place it face down in front of Jack. Place the Queen of Hearts in front of Claire.

5 Point out to Claire and Jack that from a shuffled pack Claire dealt 16 cards from which she and Jack each found a card at random, and the pack of 16 was then shuffled again by each of them. Say 'But nevertheless, if my magician's instincts are correct, I think the cards I've selected are the two you

picked out. What was your card Jack?' Jack answers 'Three of Clubs.' 'And Claire?' Claire says 'Queen of Hearts.'

6 Ask Claire and Jack to look at the cards before them and confirm that they are indeed the cards they selected.

Face to face

Skill level 2

You will need
A standard pack.

Special skills
Peeking, false shuffle.

The trick
From a shuffled pack, a card is selected and placed face up on the pack, so that everybody knows its identity. Another card is picked and placed face down on top of it. Nobody knows its identity. The magician takes the pack behind him and by touch identifies the second card.

How to do it

1 Take the pack so as to have a peek at the bottom card. Perform false shuffle 4 (see page 13) to shuffle the card to the top, and if you like perform further false shuffles to keep it there or move it to the bottom and back. In any case end so that you know the identity of the top card. Let's suppose it is the two of Clubs.

2 Place the pack on the table, cutting it so that it is in two piles. Ask a spectator, Sarah say, to choose one of the piles. If she chooses the pile with the two of Clubs on top, pick it up and discard the other. If she chooses the other, discard it and leave the half with the two of Clubs on the table.

3 Divide it into two again, saying 'I think in fact we can perform this experiment best with only a quarter of the pack, so would you indicate a pile, too, please Ian?' Ian does so, and again if he indicates the pile topped by the two

of Clubs you take it and discard the other; if he indicates the other, discard that immediately, leaving the pile topped with the two of Clubs on the table.

4 Finally you have about 13 cards on the table. Fan them out face down and ask Ian to pick a card from the fan and place it on top of the fan, and then ask him to turn it face up. Let's suppose it is the King of Diamonds. Now ask him to pick another card from the pile and without looking at it or showing it to anybody place it face down on the King of Diamonds.

5 Close up the fan and ask Sarah and Ian each to cut it. If the King of Diamonds appears on top, then ask one of them to cut it again.

6 Now take up the pile and explain what you are proposing to do. Say 'I am going to take the cards behind my back, and by feel I am going to find the King of Diamonds. It's a hard one, because there's plenty of print on the King of Diamonds, but once I've found it I'm going to trace by touch the card that is facing it, which none of us know yet. So if you'll just bear with me for a few seconds....You will realize why I used only a quarter of the pack – you wouldn't want to be waiting while I felt the faces of 50 or so cards.'

7 While you are saying this, or any other patter of your own you can invent (your own patter is always the most convincing), quietly deal the cards from your left hand to your right behind your back, as you would if you were counting them. This in effect reverses their order, so that when you've finished the King of Diamonds is actually face to face with the two of Clubs.

8 Now you can say 'Well, I've found the King of Diamonds and my fingertips tell me that the card facing it is the two of Clubs. An easy one because the shape of Clubs makes picking them quite straightforward.'

9 Bring the cards to the front and spread them face down on the table. The King of Diamonds will be face up. Withdraw the card that is face to face with it, turn it over and it will be the two of Clubs.

Ashes victory

Skill level 3

You will need
Pen and paper, ashtray, matches or lighter, access beforehand to a wet bar of soap, a prepared pack of cards.

Special skill
False shuffle.

The trick
Eight cards chosen at random are tossed face down on the table. A spectator is asked to pick up the cards and read out their names to the magician, who writes them on eight pieces of paper which he folds and places in the ashtray. The spectator picks out one and is asked to place the corresponding card face down on the table. The piece of paper is then burned. The magician takes the ashes and rubs them on his arm. The ashes form the name of a card, which turns out to be the one on the table.

How to do it

1 The chosen card has to be forced and its identity must be determined well in advance. Let us say it is the six of Clubs. Prepare your forearm by writing 6C on it with a bar of wet soap. Let this dry – it should remain active for an hour or two at least, and will remain effective beneath your sleeve.

2 Next, arrange the pack, which simply needs the six of Clubs to be the top or bottom card of the pack. This can be left to the performance – it should not be difficult for the six of Clubs to be fiddled to the bottom of the pack while you are idly playing with it and can then be falsely shuffled to the top.

3 Saying 'We need a card at random for this effect', execute any false shuffle necessary and count out eight cards face down to the table. Ask a spectator, say Bethany, to take the cards and read their names out to you while you write them on eight pieces of paper. Each piece of paper should be large enough to generate a reasonable amount of ash when it is burnt later. Whatever the cards are, do not actually write their names, merely write 'six of Clubs' on each piece of paper, folding them and placing them in the ashtray. Bethany is asked to take out one of the folded pieces of paper, open it and place the card corresponding to it face down on the table and return the other seven cards to the pack. You are not to know the chosen card.

4 Take the other unopened slips of paper from the ashtray, and if there isn't a fire to throw them into, slip them into your pocket, saying 'Obviously, I mustn't look at these, but we need the ashtray again now. Please put the slip in the ashtray, Bethany, and take the matches and set fire to it. Make sure it all gets burnt so that I cannot read it. That's right, lots of nice ash – we're going to need that, too.'

5 When the fire is out, say 'Now I'm going to try something remarkable. As you know, I had no idea which eight cards were originally dealt to the table, and there was no way I can have guessed which of the eight Bethany pulled out of the ashtray. Yet the ashes contain the essence of that card, since its name was written on the paper, and I'm going to see if that presence is strong enough to allow the ashes to indicate the name of the card on my arm.'

6 As you are saying this you are rolling up your sleeve to expose your bare forearm (on which is the dried soap). Pick up the ashes and spread them carefully on your arm. They will stick to the dry soap and fall off elsewhere, leaving the message 6C boldly written in black on your arm.

AFTERTHOUGHT

This version of the trick is more or less how it was published in a famous set of magic books which came out about 90 years ago. It has been repeated and amended in books since, but I think this version is as good as any. As the author, Mr L. Widdop, suggested, it might be even more effective if you had an accomplice who could reluctantly 'volunteer' to have the ashes rubbed on her arm while you warned of the dangers of messing about with black magic, and asked if she could feel any 'clammy, mysterious' sensations creeping up her arm and 'striking terror at the roots of her heart'.

7 Say 'It appears that the ashes contained the inner spirit of the six of Clubs. Is that the chosen card, Bethany? Please turn it over and show it to everyone. Thank you. Now if you'll excuse me for a minute or two I must go and wash the ashes of the six of Clubs from my arm.'

The short trip to the bathroom enables you to ditch the seven slips of paper that didn't get burnt.

The blackjack detective agency

Skill level 3

Special skills
Peek, false shuffle.

The trick
A spectator chooses a card at random, replaces it and it is shuffled into the pack. The two black Jacks are removed from the pack and placed on the table. Behind his back the magician inserts the two Jacks into the pack. When the pack is then looked through, the two black Jacks appear face up with a card between them. This card proves to be the spectator's chosen card.

How to do it

This is a trick with a very pleasing denouement. It is one of a class of tricks that require 'detectives' to find a certain card, and usually these detectives are Jacks, so we will use the two black Jacks. You do not announce this at first, you merely need a volunteer, let's say Zachary, to select a card at random.

1 Hand Zachary the pack and ask him to shuffle it. Take it back and square it up, taking a peek at the bottom card as you do so (see page 18). Let's say the bottom card is the two of Clubs. Fan the pack and ask Zachary to take a card from anywhere in the pack and, without letting you see it, show it to the rest of the audience. Close the pack while Zachary is doing this, then ask him to place the card back on top of the pack.

2 Now tell the audience you will give the pack a shuffle. Execute false shuffle 5 (see page 13) to ensure that Zachary's card is below the two of Clubs you peeked at, but with one change. For this trick, do not make the final cut as described, so you leave the two cards, Zachary's card and the two of Clubs, near the bottom of the pack.

3 Explain to Zachary that you are going to find his card with the help of two detectives, who will be the two black Jacks, which you must take out from the pack.

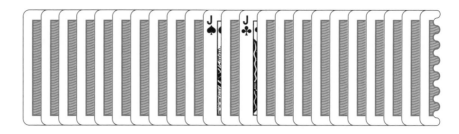

●●●●●●●●●●●●●●●

Between the two Jacks will be the audience's card.

4 Without letting the audience see the faces of the cards, riffle through the cards to look for the two black Jacks. In actual fact, you are also looking for the two of Clubs. Before throwing out the two black Jacks, you must find the two of Clubs. As you continue to riffle through, make a break in the cards with your left little finger between the two of Clubs and the card to its right, i.e. Zachary's card, (let's say it's the five of Hearts). This is made much easier by the fact that the two important cards are very close to the right-hand side of the cards as you look at them.

5 Having found the Jacks and thrown them on the table, square up the pack again, taking care to keep your little finger in the break, and in the same movement hide the pack behind your back with your left hand. Move your right hand behind your back, saying to the audience 'While holding the pack behind me, I am going to insert these two Jacks and hope that they will find Zachary's card.' While you are saying this, take the few cards below the break with your right hand behind your back and put them on top, so that the pack is now joined as one with Jack's five of Hearts as the top card of the face-down pack.

6 With the pack still behind your back, pick up one of the Jacks in your right hand and insert it face up below the top card of the pack. Then take the second Jack and place it face up on top of the pack. Still with the cards behind your back cut the cards somewhere around the middle, bring the bottom half over the top so that the Jacks and five of Hearts are in the middle, and bring the pack back to the front.

7 Spread the cards face down on the table. The two Jacks will be face up in the centre with a card face down between them (see above). Say to Zachary 'The detectives appear to think that this is your card, Zachary', pointing to the face-down card between them. 'What was your card?' When Zachary answers 'The five of Hearts', ask him to turn the card over and he will expose the five of Hearts.

More advanced magic

Jumping Jacks

Skill level 3

You will need
A standard pack.

Special skills
Double lift.

The trick
Four Jacks are shown and laid face down on the table. The magician inserts three of them in different positions in the pack. Each time the Jack appears at a click to jump from one position to another. When placed in the pack the final Jack performs a somersault and turns face up.

How to do it

1 Fan through the face-up pack and throw the four Jacks to the table, so that everyone can see them.

2 Turn the pack over in your hand, and pick up the Jacks with your right hand, place them face up on top of the pack. Fan them out and show them to the audience, holding them in your left hand with the rest of the pack behind them and the top two or three face-down cards also slightly fanned out. This enables you to establish a break between the first and second face-down cards with the little finger of your left hand.

3 Square up the pack again, at the same time transferring the break to your right thumb, and in the same movement lift off the four Jacks with the top face-down card behind them. This is an adaptation of the double lift (see page 16). You now have five cards in your right hand, which you should be holding palm downwards. Be careful not to let the audience see the bottom card of the five, which is face down.

4 As you are doing all this, tell the audience that Jacks are also known as knaves and that knaves are naughty persons. Say 'Have you heard of a jumping jack? It's a name given to a firework that jumps about the floor when it's lit. The cards called Jacks also jump about a bit, as I hope to show. Here are the four little rascals.'

5 You now replace the cards in your right hand face down onto the pack as follows. Holding the pack in the dealing position in your left hand, and the Jacks in your right hand, pull the first Jack from the pile with your left thumb so it overlaps the main pack. Announce its rank and suit ('Here we have the Jack of Spades') and use the remaining cards in your right hand to tip the Jack face down onto the pack. The technique is explained with diagrams in the trick The four aces (see page 100). Repeat this with the following two Jacks. When you reach the fourth Jack (with the face-down card below it) just put it face up on the pack (keeping the card hidden below it), announce its identity and then turn just the Jack over. The top of the pack now consists of Jack, ordinary card, Jack, Jack, Jack.

6 Now tell the audience you are going to place the four Jacks face down on the table. Of course, one of the four cards is not a Jack, and it must be the fourth card in the row. So lay down the first card a little to your right, the second card (the non-Jack) a little to its right. Then, as if you are going too far to the right, place the third card to the left of the first, and the fourth card to the left of that.

7 Say 'Now I'm going to make them jump! Let's take this first one. I'll put him on the bottom of the pack, like so...' Place the pack on top of the Jack at the left end of the row, and pick the whole pack up again. Riffle the pack and turn over the top card. It is, of course, a Jack. Say 'As I thought, he's jumped straight to the top of the pack!' Take this Jack and place it face up on the table, beginning a new row.

8 Pick up the second card on the table (without showing its face to the audience). Place it face down on top of the pack. Riffle the cards and say 'I wouldn't be surprised if this one doesn't jump straight to the bottom...' Take the pack in your right hand, turn it over and put it back in your left. Sure enough, there is a Jack showing. Take this Jack and place it face up beside the other face-up Jack.

9 Pick up the third face-down card from the table and say 'This Jack I'll put into the middle of the pack. He'll be clever if he can jump from there.' Hold up the pack in your left hand at eye level, holding it sideways between the tip of your thumb and the tips of your extended fingers, so that the audience can see you insert the Jack in the middle. Some of them might forget that the pack is actually face up. When you've done this, use your thumb to turn the pack over as you let it drop into your palm, so that it is now face down as you riffle the pack and say 'Let's see if he's managed to get to the top from there.' Turn over the top card, and there again is the Jack. Say 'I told you there was no limit to the tricks of these cunning fellows.'

10 Saying 'Let's see what surprise this last one may have for us', pick up the last face-down card, which *you* know, of course, isn't a Jack. Hold up the face-down pack at eye level in your left hand again and insert the final card in the middle. This time you can tilt the pack towards the audience, so that they can see the backs of the cards and the fact that the card being inserted is face down like the others.

11 Returning the pack to your palm, give it a riffle and say 'Has this Jack leapt to the top?' and turn over the top card. It is not a Jack. Replace it. 'Is he at the bottom?' Turn over the pack. 'No, he isn't. Where is he then?' Fan out the cards face up so that the audience can see the faces. In the centre is a face-down card. Say 'Could this be Jack?' and withdraw the card, showing its face to the audience. It is, indeed, the final Jack. Say 'Well, that was a terrific effort. The little rascal has performed a somersault and jumped clean over. What an entertaining group these Jacks are!'

It's all going wrong

Skill level 3

You will need
A standard pack.

Special skills
False shuffle.

The trick
While the magician's back is turned, a spectator shuffles the pack. He then thinks of a number between one and ten, silently counts down to that number, looks at that card and remembers it. He hands the pack to another spectator, who thinks of a number between 11 and 20 and does the same. The pack is then handed to the magician behind his back. The magician turns and announces he is going to find the spectators' cards while the pack is behind his back.

He produces a card, which is a wrong card. With the pack now in front of him, he asks the first spectator which number he thought of, counts down, and produces another card. Wrong again. In despair, he turns to the second spectator and asks the number of his card. Counting down, the magician produces a card for that spectator. For the third time he is wrong. He shuffles the pack, and offering it to the second spectator asks her to cut the cards. She takes half the cards and places them on the table. The magician places his half of the cards criss-cross fashion on top of the other half. When the magician turns over the top pile and the top card of the pile below, the chosen cards of the two spectators are revealed.

How to do it

Everybody loves the magician who appears to bumble from mistake to mistake only to produce a surprising twist at the end, which shows that everything was under control after all. The great entertainer Tommy Cooper made an art form of his apparent clumsiness.

1 Hand the pack to a spectator, say David, and ask him to shuffle it thoroughly. When he has done so, ask him to think of a number between one and ten without telling you what it is. Say to him 'I am now going to turn my back. Without me seeing, silently count down to the card corresponding to the number you thought of, look at it and remember what it is. Don't take it out – leave it where it is in the pack. Tell me when you've done that.'

2 When David has completed his job, turn round and ask him to give the pack to another spectator – let's say her name is Molly. Say 'Now, Molly, you must think of a number between 11 and 20, and when I turn my back you must do as David did, that is count down to the card in that position, look at it and remember it. Please do not disturb the order of the cards. What I am going to try to do is remarkable enough as it is – if you upset the order of the cards it would need a miracle-worker to do it.'

3 When Molly has done as asked, keep your back to the audience and ask her to put the cards face down in your hands. When you have the cards in your hands turn to face the audience, keeping your hands behind you.

4 'What I propose to do', you say, 'is find both your cards behind my back. The first one, I think, is not too difficult. This, I think, is the card you chose, David. Am I right?'

5 You bring your hands to the front, the face-down pack in your left hand and an odd card in your right, which you lay face down on the table. David says 'No, that's not my card.' You look bewildered.

6 In fact, you know it is not David's card. What you do behind your back while addressing the audience, is to take one card from the bottom of the pack and place it face down on the top. You then take a second card from the bottom of the pack, and this is the one you produce as David's card.

7 When David denies it, and you have looked suitably embarrassed, put the wrong card on the bottom of the pack and then ask David what number it was that he originally thought of. Let us say David says 'Six.'

8 Count off five cards face down on the table and turn up the sixth face up. Say 'Then this was your card, David?' David says 'No, wrong again.' Look completely baffled and ask David if he is sure. He will tell you he is absolutely sure and that you've messed up the trick.

In fact, all that these manoeuvrings have achieved so far is that David's chosen card is now on top of the pile in your left hand.

9 Say, 'Oh, well, let's see if we can find Molly's card. Let's see, we've got six cards here.' Place these six cards on the bottom of the pack. 'What was the number you thought of Molly?' Suppose Molly says 'Seventeen.'

10 Start dealing cards from the top of the pack face down onto the table, counting as you go, starting at seven. Turning over the seventeenth card, say to Molly 'Then that's your card, Molly.' Molly says 'No – it's just not your day is it.'

11 Put the face-up card on top of the pile and put the pile on the bottom of the pack, looking suitably crestfallen. Say 'I might have had better luck if I'd just given the whole pack a complete shuffle in the first place.' With that, shuffle the pack.

If you have been following this with the cards in your hand, you will know that the situation with the pack before you shuffle is that David's card is the bottom card of the pack and Molly's is the top. Your shuffle must retain this situation, so you use false shuffle 6 (see page 14).

12 Offering the pack to Molly, ask her to cut it somewhere near the middle and put the top half of the pack face down on the table. Place your half of the pack crossways on top of it.

13 Say to David 'Out of interest, David, what was your card?' Suppose David says 'The three of Diamonds.' Turn over the top of the two criss-cross piles. The top card is the three of Diamonds. Say 'Well, would you believe it, Molly has cut the cards exactly at your card. That hardly seems possible. What was your card Molly?' Suppose she says 'Ace of Clubs.'

14 Taking the top card of the face-down pack say 'I suppose it would be too much to expect this to be the Ace of Clubs.' Turn it over. It is the Ace of Clubs.

TIP

What the audience will not spot is that although your two helpers each counted out an unknown number of cards while your back was turned, you actually asked David and Molly what those numbers were before you produced the respective cards. So the final production of the two chosen cards was not all that clever. The initial slight meddling with the pack behind your back at the beginning allowed you to produce the wrong cards to start with and then later to produce the correct ones. All the rest is hocus-pocus, and the success of the trick relies on how well you convince your audience that things are going wrong. Do not ham it up, just look perplexed and quietly desperate all through. Your triumph comes at the end. The trick is simple – the performance everything.

More advanced magic

The four Aces

Skill level 4

You will need
A standard pack.

Special skills
Double lift, false shuffle.

The trick
The four Aces are laid on the table, face up. A spectator chooses one out loud and the Aces are returned to the top of the pile. The magician then deals the four Aces face down to the table, beginning with the spectator's chosen Ace, and adds three face-down cards to each, making four piles. The pile on the Ace chosen by the spectator is given to her to hold. The magician turns over the other three piles card by card and the Aces have disappeared. They turn up in the spectator's hand.

How to do it
The trick with the four Aces is a popular one which has appeared in a number of books with slightly different ways of doing it, even to the use of a shortened card. I prefer to use a standard pack.

1 Openly remove from the pack the four Aces and lay them face up on the table. Ask a spectator, let's call her Hannah (a younger kid is a good helper for this trick), to name her favourite Ace. While you are talking and she is thinking, casually be squaring up the pack, which disguises your real purpose, to count down three cards from the top of the pack and establish a break with your little finger.

2 When Hannah chooses her favourite Ace – let's suppose it is the Ace of Diamonds – pick it up and place it face up on top of the pack in your left hand. Then pick up the other three Aces and place them face up on the pack, at the same time lifting off with your right hand the cards above your finger break.

3 In your right hand you now hold a pile of seven cards consisting of the four Aces face up and below three ordinary cards face down. You now say to the audience 'Now remember the order in which I place these four Aces on the pack because I want you to remember in which order I am going to deal them in a minute to the table.'

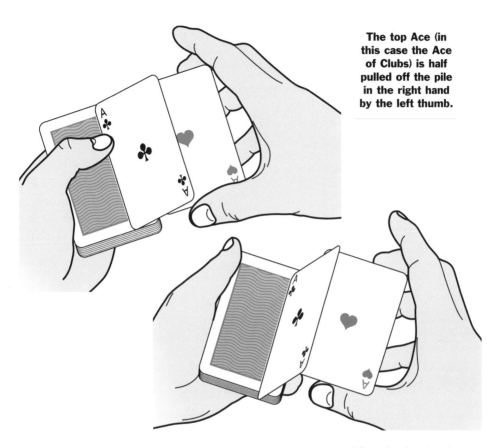

The top Ace (in this case the Ace of Clubs) is half pulled off the pile in the right hand by the left thumb.

After the Ace has been half pulled from the pile, the cards in the right hand are used to tip it over face down onto the main pack.

4 Let us say the order of the Aces is Clubs, Hearts, Spades, with at the bottom Hannah's choice, Diamonds.

5 Bring the right hand across to the left. Throughout the following moves you have to keep the right-hand pile closely into your palm so that the audience cannot see that you have face-down cards at the bottom.

6 With your hands close together, half pull off the top Ace with your left thumb and saying 'Ace of Clubs', use the right-hand cards to tip it over face down onto the pack (see above). Do the same with the next card, saying 'Ace of Hearts', and the third, saying 'Ace of Spades'. The audience can see the faces of these cards as you flick them over. Now you have in your right hand the Ace of Diamonds on top of three face-down cards, whose presence the audience do not suspect.

7 Do not attempt anything complicated here. Just place the four cards without fuss on top of the pack with the Ace of Diamonds face up. Show the pack to the audience showing the Ace and saying 'And of course on the top is Hannah's card, the Ace of Diamonds.'

More advanced magic

8 You can now turn the Ace of Diamonds face down and relax, because all the hard work is already done.

9 Say, 'I am now going to lay down the Aces in a line. The first one, as we know, is the Ace of Diamonds. I've forgotten what the second, third and fourth Aces are, but I'm sure you've all remembered and you can demonstrate how good your memory is in a moment.'

10 As you are talking, deal the top four cards face down in a row. Say 'Now, I'm going to add three cards to the top of each Ace.' Do so, adding three cards to each 'Ace' in turn. Square up the piles and say to Hannah 'Now I'm sure, Hannah, you know which pile has the Ace of Diamonds on the bottom.' If Hannah has forgotten, the audience will tell her. It is the first pile of course.

11 Pick up the first pile and turn it over, showing the audience the Ace of Diamonds, now on top. Say to Hannah 'Hold out your left hand.' Place the pile on Hannah's palm and tell her to put her right hand on top. 'Hold these for a minute or two Hannah and don't let anybody take them.'

12 Point to the second pile and say to the audience 'Who can remember which Ace is at the bottom of this pile?' Many in the audience will call out 'The Ace of Spades.'

13 Take up the pile and deal the cards one by one to the table calling out each card as you do so, e.g. 'Three of Hearts, Jack of Clubs, four of Hearts and, of course, the Ace of Spades.' But when you turn the final card over it is not an Ace at all. Say 'Well, where has the Ace gone? It has disappeared. Let's see if we have better luck with this pile. Which Ace is at the bottom?' With luck, a couple of the audience will say 'Ace of Hearts.' Go through the same routine, and discover that the Ace of Hearts has disappeared, too.

14 Taking up the last pile say 'Well, I suppose the card at the bottom of this pile should be the Ace of Clubs, but the way things are going, I do not suppose anybody's willing to bet on it. I thought not.' Go through the cards one by one again to find the fourth Ace has also disappeared.

15 Say 'I wonder where all the Aces have gone. I suppose you haven't taken them, have you Hannah?'

16 This is why I like a young person to hold the cards, because most of the audience will by now expect Hannah to be holding all the Aces.

17 Ask Hannah to show which cards she has, and of course they are the four Aces.

More advanced magic

Divination

Skill level 3

You will need
A standard pack, four small pieces of paper, two pens.

The trick
A member of the audience shuffles the pack and deals out ten pairs of cards face down. With the magician's back turned, two other spectators pick one of the pairs of cards each and write down the names of the two cards making up their pair on separate pieces of paper. The slips of paper are folded up, and the pairs of cards returned to the table. A fourth spectator collects the pairs of cards in any order he wishes and the magician turns round and takes the 20 cards. He throws them one at a time haphazardly onto the table, then arranges them in a rectangle and turns them face up. The onlookers with the folded slips of paper put the slips against the rows containing their cards. One by one the magician picks up each slip, moves it along the row and, like a water diviner, detects activity in the slip of paper when it passes over the appropriate card. The cards and the slips are put to one side and found to match.

How to do it
This trick requires no special sleight-of-hand skills, but it relies for its effect entirely on the ease with which it is performed. You need to remember four words and to make one difficult move with apparent casualness, while in fact concentrating hard.

1 The pack is given to an onlooker, say Sam. He is asked to give the cards a thorough shuffle and to deal out ten piles of two cards each, face down. Take the rest of the pack and put it to one side, saying 'As you can see, I have no idea which cards are dealt or how they are paired up. In fact, Sam, if you want to change over any cards to make new pairs, please do so.'

2 Hand two slips of paper and a pen to each of two other onlookers. Let's call them Ryan and Louise. Ideally one should be to your left and one to your right. Say 'Now I'm going to turn my back. I want you, Ryan, and you, Louise, to select one of the pairs of cards each, write down on the slips of paper the two cards in the pair and then return the pair of cards face down to the table. You needn't put it in the same place as you picked it up; if you like you can swap its

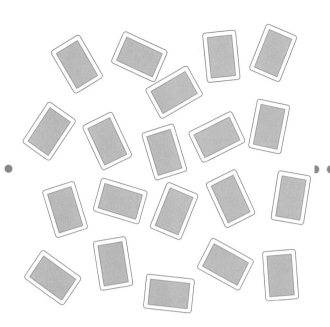

How the cards might be scattered 'haphazardly', although you, in fact, know they are in four rows of five, and arranged in a definite pattern.

position with any other pair. Fold the slips of paper containing the cards' names and hold them in your hand. I mustn't know what cards you picked. Have you done that?'

3 When this operation has been carried out, ask Sam, or even a fourth member of the audience, to collect up one by one the ten pairs of cards. Say 'Pick them up in any order you like, but please keep them in their pairs.'

4 Once Sam has done this, turn round and take the cards from him and begin throwing them one by one on the table. This is where the great skill comes in. You must start doing this, and after three or four cards say 'What I'm doing now is throwing the cards down haphazardly on the table so that the pairs get well separated, and the cards that Ryan and Louise selected get well and truly mixed up in the general hodge-podge.'

5 In fact you are throwing the cards down in a careful pattern, a very rough rectangle, corresponding to four five-letter words. These four words contain ten pairs of letters and you throw the cards in pairs according to the pairs of letters, which are not duplicated. The words represent your key and the order in which you throw down the cards corresponds to them as follows:

First row –	TOAST	1 3 5 7 2
Second row –	PAPER	9 6 10 11 13
Third row –	OCCUR	4 15 16 17 14
Fourth row –	DUDES	19 18 20 12 8

As you can see, the first pair of cards thrown down corresponds to the two 'T's in 'toast', the second to the 'O's in 'toast' and 'occur'.

6 When you've finished, say 'Having scattered the cards around, I'll now tidy them up into a square, or more correctly, a rectangle.' Having done this, say 'Now I'll turn the cards face up'.

More advanced magic

The illustration opposite shows how you might throw down the cards in the first place, and the one below shows the tidied-up rectangle with the cards turned face up.

7 Once you've completed this operation successfully, and nobody has suspected that the cards are in a thought-out pattern, you can relax. The hard work is done. Now say 'Ryan, look at your slips of paper, fold them back up so I can't see them and put each of them down next to the row in which the card it represents is placed. And Louise,

would you do the same, please? Ryan, you put your slips this side, and Louise you put yours this side.'

8 While Ryan and Louise are doing this, remind the audience of what has happened and tell them what you are going to do. Say 'Remember, these 20 cards were dealt in pairs from a shuffled pack, and Ryan and Louise chose their pairs without me seeing which pairs they took. In fact, I didn't touch the cards until I spread them out on the table. You'll agree I cannot possibly know the identities of the four

How the cards appear 'tidied up' and turned over. The asterisks represent the slips of paper placed against the rows by Louise and Ryan (see page 106).

cards Ryan and Louise chose. What I propose to do is discover them by divination. You all know how water diviners discover water by the way their divining rod twitches when water is below it. I am going to find the cards by passing the slips over them and hopefully detecting some reaction when a slip passes over the correct card. This is not easy, so wish me luck.'

You will notice that each of the four words in your key contains two identical letters, so it is possible that the two slips of paper that either of your helpers hold will be placed against the same row. The asterisks in the illustration on the previous page represent the slips of paper that Ryan (to the left) and Louise (to the right) have placed against the layout. Louise's two cards are both in the same row. You know Louise's cards are the first and third, representing the 'P' in 'paper', in other words, the six of Diamonds and five of Clubs.

9 Pick up the two slips in the palm of one hand and pass your hand over the whole row. Then repeat the operation slowly. When passing over one of Louise's cards, say 'I think I got a reaction then. Yes, this is definitely one of the cards.' Pick it up and throw it onto the table in front of Louise. Pass over the cards again and say 'And I'm sure this is the other', picking up and passing

the other card towards Louise, putting it on top of the first. Without unfolding them, put the two slips of paper on top and say 'Now I'll deal with Ryan's cards. This should be easier because as they're in separate rows I should get a clearer signal.' You know Ryan's cards represent the letter 'S' in 'toast' and 'Dudes' so picking up the slip opposite the top row you can pretend to get a reaction over the fourth card.

10 Take out Ryan's card and place it in front of him with the folded slip on top of it, and do the same with his other card. Ask Ryan and Louise to unfold their slips of paper and confirm that you are, indeed, a good diviner.

Notice that with Ryan's cards, you could marry up each slip with its appropriate card, but with Louise's, because they were in the same row, you couldn't. If you get both pairs of cards in separate rows, excellent – that is the best outcome. If, as in the example, you get one pair in the same row, deal with that first, saving your best effect to last. If both sets are in the same row – well, it's still an impressive trick!

Card and number matching

Skill level 3

Skill level 3

You will need
A standard pack.

Special skills
False shuffles, the glide.

The trick
One member of the audience shuffles, and then picks and remembers a card from a fanned-out pack. The pack is then cut into two and the spectator is asked to replace her card on top of whichever piles she prefers. This pile is then shuffled and another member of the audience is asked to name a number from one to twenty-five. Cards are dealt face down from the bottom of the pack until this number is reached. The spectator who chose the card is then asked to name it and is asked to turn over the card just dealt. It turns out to be the card she chose.

How to do it
For this trick you will need to be comfortable with the glide (see page 15), since you are going to deal a number of cards from the bottom of the pack while actually holding on to the bottom card. You also need two of the false shuffles.

1 When the spectator, say Julia, has taken her card, divide the pack as near as you can by sight into two and place the two halves face down on the table. Ask Julia to remember her card and place it face down on either pile. Put the other pile to one side and pick up the pile with Julia's card on top. Tell the audience you will shuffle the cards thoroughly, and execute false shuffle 3 (see page 12) to take the card to the bottom, and then do false shuffle 2 a couple of times (see page 12) to keep it there.

2 Then ask another member of the audience, say Richard, to choose a number between one and twenty-four. Tell him you divided the pack into two to save time and that you reckon you've got about 24 cards in your pile. Let's suppose Richard says 'Fifteen.'

● ● ● ● ● ● ● ● ● ● ● ● ● ● ● ● ●

3 While you have been talking to Richard you have arranged the cards in your left hand, palm down, in order to execute the glide (see page 15). In fact by the time you have finished talking with Richard, your left-hand little finger has pulled the bottom card of the pack (Julia's card) well back into your palm (a couple of centimetres or so if you can manage it).

4 Tell the audience that you are now going to deal cards off the bottom of the pack until you reach Richard's number. In fact you keep dealing the second-bottom card from the pack, counting out loud as you go, until you actually reach Richard's number, when you deal the actual bottom card, which is, of course, the card Julia originally selected.

5 You then say to the audience 'I am hoping that this is the card which Julia originally picked at random from the whole pack. If you remember that card was thoroughly shuffled into this half of the pack, and Richard gave us a number of his choice, actually 15. This is the fifteenth card I've dealt. It will be an extraordinary coincidence if Richard has found Julia's card, but that's what I'm hoping for. Now, what was your card, Julia?'

When dealing from the bottom of the pack, keep the pack well squared up. If you start pulling the bottom cards forward, tap them back into place. You do not want to have them protruding when the time comes to take the real bottom card, as you'll have to reach well back for it, which might make what you're doing obvious. When you are transferring the last false card to the table, push the real bottom card forward with your little finger so that you can deal it onto the table quite naturally. Although it sounds unlikely, an easy mistake to make is to get so confidently into the groove of dealing the second-bottom card, that when you need to deal the real one you forget and take the second-bottom card again.

6 Julia names her card, and you ask her to turn over the card you've just dealt to the table. It is her card.

More advanced magic

Three-card trick

• •

Skill level 4

You will need
A standard pack, a second pack from which to make a false Queen, sticky tape, scissors.

Special skills
Palming, the glide and double lift.

The trick
The audience are shown three cards, one of which is a Queen. The magician manipulates the cards and asks a spectator to pick the Queen from three face-down cards. By the use of deception by the magician, the spectator, who thinks he knows which is the Queen, finds that he has got it wrong.

• •

How to do it
There are many ways of doing the famous Three-card Trick, known professionally as the Three-card Monte, and also popularly called Find the Lady. Here is a little routine that allows you to do it in three different ways. One way needs a prepared pack, so can be performed only once, and must come first.

Using a prepared pack
1 You need to take a Queen – let's use the Queen of Hearts – from an identical pack and cut about 2.5cm (1in) from the top. Cut a similar piece from another card (or the other end of the Queen would do) and hinge the two pieces together with sticky tape (see below), with the tape inside the hinge.

A hinged Queen of Hearts made from a card from another pack to fit over an ordinary card as shown for the three-card trick.

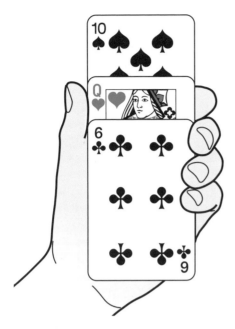

How to show
the cards to
the audience.

5 Draw off the second card, which everybody will think is the Queen, but hold the hinged part back in your left hand. Place the card on the table then withdraw the third one, completing the row of three on the table. The hinged piece of card is a convenient size and shape to be palmed in your hand, which you drop casually to your side.

6 Ask somebody to pick the Queen of Hearts and turn the card over. Obviously they will be wrong. Somebody else can have a try – wrong again. Now ask one of the young members of your audience to turn over the third card, saying something like 'Now Sophie, *you* show them how it's done – you find the Queen.' Of course, Sophie will get it wrong, too. Say 'Oh dear, where can the Queen have got to then?'

7 You now casually put your left hand in your pocket and say 'I'm not surprised you didn't find the lady, Sophie, because look, here she is in my pocket all the time.' As you take the Queen out of your pocket, replace it with the hinged piece of card (this is why the Queen has to be in the left pocket). When you've shown the Queen of Hearts all round you can add it to the rest of the cards and you have a regular pack again to move on to the next phase of this three-part routine.

2 Take the Queen from the pack you are going to use and place it in your left pocket. Then slip the hinged piece over the top of a plain card from the main pack, and place this fake Queen between two other plain cards (I think it's best to use black number cards, so that the Queen is quite different from the others).

3 When you produce the pack, fan through it and take out the three cards and show them to the audience in your left hand with the 'Queen' in the centre, as in the illustration above. Make sure that the 'Queen' lines up exactly with the other cards and that nobody can tell it isn't the genuine Queen of Hearts.

4 When your audience have all had a good view of it, close the three cards together, turn your palm downwards, so that the cards are face down, and then with the right hand draw off the top card and lay it face down on the table.

How to hold the Queen of Hearts.

Repeating the trick

If asked to repeat the trick, do not refuse, just pick up the Queen of Hearts and two plain cards, and say 'OK, watch.'

1 You can let the audience examine the cards if they wish. Place the Queen in your right hand, held between your thumb and your index finger, which grasp the card towards the left of the Queen as the audience looks at it (see top right). Bend the card a little so that it curves in slightly. Say 'Queen.'

2 Take the next card (let's assume it's the ten of Spades) and hold it in front of the Queen with the thumb at the bottom and the middle and third finger at the top, again slightly concave (see right). Say 'Ten.' Take the third card (let's say it's the six of Clubs) and hold it similarly in the left hand between the thumb and second and third fingers. Say 'Six.'

3 Wave your arms a little and suddenly drop them towards the table, palms downwards so that nobody sees the faces of the cards, throwing the Queen onto the table from right to left. With practice you will find it very easy to do this without dropping the other card (ten of Spades in this case) or letting it get in the way of the Queen.

The Queen and ten as the audience sees them.

As you draw back your right hand the left comes across and throws the six of Clubs face down on the table towards the right. Then, as you pull back your left hand, your right hand drops the ten of Spades in the centre between the other two cards. This is all done very fast and all the time you make sure that the faces of the cards are not raised – your audience must not see them.

4 As soon as the three cards are down, use both hands to change quickly the places of the cards in the centre and on the right by sliding them

More advanced magic

111

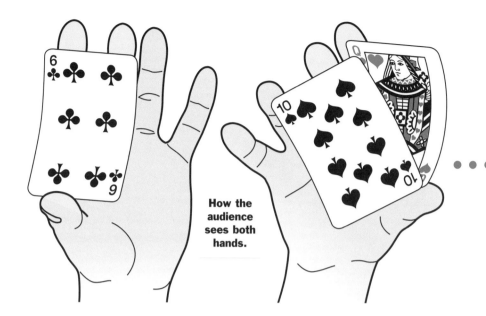

How the audience sees both hands.

clockwise from nine o'clock to three o'clock and vice versa. The audience will almost universally believe that the first card you released from your right hand was the ten of Spades and the Queen was therefore dropped in the centre and is now on the right.

5 Ask one member of the audience, say Ben, to find the lady and to turn over his choice of card. Do not allow everybody to choose as somebody is bound to pick the correct card. Once Ben has chosen wrongly, pick up all three cards as if you've finished with this trick.

6 However, if pressed, be persuaded to do the trick again, but this time swap the positions of the Queen and ten, throwing down the ten first. This time the Queen *will* be dropped in the middle and be switched to the right. Whoever is asked to find the lady will almost always pick the left-hand card. If they don't and happen to find the Queen congratulate them and say 'Let's try again.' Never try the trick a third time,

as someone will spot what's going on. Just switch without explanation to the third phase.

The last trick

1 Show the three cards around. Let's assume you're using the same three. Let people examine them, then fan them face up in your left hand with the Queen on top (see opposite, top). When everybody's seen them, give the cards a couple of shuffles, but keep the Queen on top. Square up the cards. Make sure the cards are well squared up top, bottom and sides, otherwise the next moves will be spotted. After each operation square up the cards carefully.

2 Take the cards in your left hand, the palm facing downwards, with the cards held along one long edge by the index finger and along the other by the thumb (see opposite, middle). The second and third fingers lightly touch the back of the bottom card, somewhere

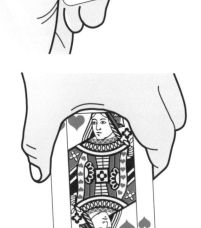

Show the audience the three cards.

near the centre. You now perform two of the moves from the front of the book, the glide (see page 15) and the double lift (see page 16).

3 Holding the cards lightly, your second and third fingers slide the bottom card back towards the palm about a centimetre or so. With your right thumb on top of the Queen and first two fingers below the second card, execute the double lift (see bottom right). This takes the Queen and the second card away, exposing the bottom card – let's say it's the six of Clubs. The audience can see that and the Queen, but they think you have only the top card in your right hand, and the other two in your left.

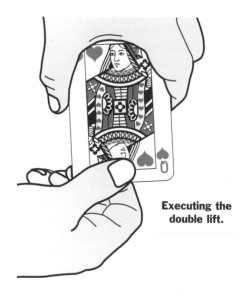

Holding the three cards with the Queen uppermost.

4 Now turn both hands over so that the cards are face down, as you do so extending your left index finger around the top of the card in your left hand, pushing it into your palm so that the audience cannot see that it is only a single card. Slide the two face-down cards from your right hand over the card in your left. If done quickly and neatly, nobody will spot the double lift. Now turn your left hand over again so that the audience can see the six of Clubs on top. The Queen is now of course in the middle, but the audience thinks it's at the bottom. Square the cards.

Executing the double lift.

More advanced magic ♠

5 Repeat the glide and double lift as before, exposing the ten of Spades, which confirms the audience's impression – that the ten of Spades was the middle card. Now when you turn the cards over the Queen has come to the top, although the audience thinks it's in the middle. Fan the cards out face down and ask another member of the audience, say Jack, to take the Queen. He will pick the centre card, and be amazed when it's the six of Clubs.

6 If pressed you can do this again – it will usually stand a repeat performance. Say after the first operation 'I put the Queen on the bottom.' After the second operation, 'I now put the six on the bottom.' Do not do the glide and double lift a third time with the cards face up as you'll expose the Queen. But you can turn the cards over and repeat the operation face down. The audience think the Queen is in the middle, remember, so there's no need now to execute the double lift. Just take the top card and slide it to the bottom. As you do so, let your left thumb push the second card slightly inwards toward the palm, so that the audience see that you have two cards in your left hand. Choose another member of the audience, fan the cards out and say 'Now, where's the Queen, Jade?' If she's been paying attention, Jade now takes

the top card – the Queen is actually the bottom card.

7 Thank all those of your audience who've assisted you by failing to find the Queen and refuse, if asked, to perform the trick again, saying 'That's enough of the Queen of Hearts. Let her get on with baking tarts while we try something else.'

More advanced magic

The wrong card

Skill level 4

You will need
A standard pack of cards.

Special skills
The roly-poly pass, false shuffles, double lift.

The trick
A spectator shuffles a pack, and the magician fans it out and asks him to take a card, look at it and remember it. It is then placed back in the centre of the pack, which is given a further good shuffle. The magician takes the pack behind his back and brings it back with a card in his right hand and the rest in his left. He shows the card to the spectator who says it isn't his card. Looking puzzled, the magician lays it face down while he has another try. He is again wrong. After being wrong a third time, the magician asks the spectator what his card was. The magician looks for it in his pack but cannot find it. It transpires it is the card on the table, which the spectator has denied was his. It has mysteriously changed from the wrong card into the correct card.

How to do it

1 Ask a spectator (let's call him Alex) to shuffle the pack thoroughly and hand it back to you. Thank him, fan the pack out and ask him to choose a card, look at it and remember it. We'll assume it's the Jack of Hearts. While he is doing this, separate the pack into two halves (it's most naturally done at the point where Alex took his card) and ask Alex to place his card face down on the pack in your left hand. There is no need to peek at any cards.

2 When Alex has returned his card, execute the roly-poly pass (see page 22), which brings Alex's card to the top of the pack. In the same movement continue with false shuffles 3 and 4 (see pages 12–13). These take Alex's card to the bottom of the pack and then back to the top again. Do not let anybody see the face of Alex's card in its progress from top to bottom.

3 Say to the audience 'Now Alex picked his card at will from a pack he shuffled himself. He put it back into the centre of the pack that has again been thoroughly shuffled. Alex's card, which only he and you know, could be anywhere in the pack. What I am going to do now, behind my back, is to find his card.'

4 Take the cards behind your back. Alex's card is, of course, the top one, but what you do is to take the top two cards in a double lift (see page 16). Don't forget you are supposed to be searching for Alex's card, so you have plenty of time to line up the two cards in your right hand, using your left thumb and fingers. I prefer to hold the two cards with my thumb at bottom and just my middle finger at the top, with my index finger touching the back of the cards. The cards can be slightly bent, either backwards or forwards if you feel it helps to keep them together, but only slightly – you have to lay them back on top of the pack and a bend would be noticeable.

5 Bringing the double-lifted cards to the front in your right hand, and the pack to the front in your left, confidently show the exposed card to Alex and say 'I believe this is your card.' At the same time lay the face-down pack on the table.

6 Alex will, of course, say it isn't his card. Resist the temptation to look at it yourself. Drop your head and look puzzled. Say 'That's funny – how did that happen?' After a moment's thought say 'Let me have another try.' Add the 'card' to the top of the pack and take the pack up again. Without making it obvious let everybody see that you're not meddling with the cards. The audience must be certain that the wrong card is now at the top of the pack – in reality Alex's card is.

7 Before taking the cards behind your back again, have what seems to be an afterthought. Lay the top card on the table face down, saying 'Well, we don't want this one – let's reject that.'

8 From behind your back produce in your right hand another card. Beware: this obviously mustn't be the card from the top of the pack that has already been seen – the audience think that one is on the table. I find it best, while the pack is behind my back, to bury this top card in the middle of the pack, so that there is no danger I produce it again.

9 Now you can safely take the top card again, and bring it round as before, showing it, in exactly the same manner as the first time, to Alex. Say, confidently, 'This must be it.' Again Alex says no. Look a bit exasperated now, and throw this card onto the table on top of the other. Say 'One more try – I'm bound to get it right this time.'

10 Go through the exercise again, throwing the third wrong card on the previous two. Say 'I cannot believe it. What was your card?'

11 Alex says the Jack of Hearts. Look through all the cards in your hand twice. Say 'Well, it's not here. Whatever happened to it?'

12 Flick over the three cards you've thrown on the table. The bottom one will be the Jack of Hearts. You now pretend indignation. Say 'Look, it was the first card I showed you. You've been messing me about.' Alex and the audience will say 'No, that wasn't the card you showed us.' Perhaps they will name the actual card you first showed them. In which case you can look through the cards in your hand and say 'No it wasn't – that's here in the middle of the pack, look.'

13 By now, of course, most of the audience will realize they've been tricked by a smart operator. You needn't admit it. As you pick up the cards say something like 'Oh, well, you live and learn. I'll choose my audiences more carefully in future.'

OBSERVATIONS

The trick works much better because you did not look at the first card you showed Alex. If you had, you could not show such fake indignation at the end because, like the audience, you would 'know' the Jack of Hearts wasn't the card you showed them.

Once you have managed to get Alex's card on the table, you can relax and pay attention to your patter. You must obviously take care that you do not produce the same wrong card a second time. Also, when you are showing the second and third wrong cards, although you have not double-lifted and have only one card in your hand, show them to the audience in exactly the same way as the first one, to lower the audience's suspicions. It's little details like these that sort out the good magicians.
You must also be alert in case anybody tries to turn face up the card on the table, thus exposing it as Alex's card, while the trick is in progress. You must be ready to stop that and say 'We'll come to that later.'

What happened to the burglars?

Skill level 3

You will need
A standard pack.

Special skill
The double lift.

The trick
The audience is reminded of the earlier trick called The four burglars (see page 32) and the magician promises to let the audience know their fate. The four Jacks are thrown onto the table, and placed face down on the top of the pack, which now represents the garden. They split up, with one Jack going south (the bottom of the pack – the audience is shown that it is indeed a Jack which goes here). Another goes east (this Jack is put two-thirds of the way down the pack), a third west (this Jack is placed a third of the way down) and the fourth north (this Jack, shown to the audience, remains on top of the pack). Members of the audience, representing policemen, cut the pack as often as they like. Finally the pack is fanned out to discover the four Jacks all together in their meeting place, the local pub.

How to do it
This trick should not be performed unless The four burglars (page 32) has already been performed successfully. It makes a good complement to The four burglars, but should not be performed if The four burglars was performed after Jumping jacks, as suggested on page 34. Three tricks about the cunning properties of the four Jacks would be too much.

1 Begin by reminding the audience of the exploits of the four burglars in the earlier trick. Remind them that the situation of the burglars at the end of that trick was that three were on the roof about to make their way down the fire escape to join their lookout friend in the garden.

2 While reminding the audience of this, fan through the pack and throw the four Jacks onto the table. As you finish your patter you square up the pack in your left hand and establish a break with your little finger below the top two cards. Pick up the four Jacks with your right hand and place them face up on top of the face-down pack. At the same time transfer the break to your right thumb and lift off the top six cards with your right hand (you now hold in your right hand four Jacks face up followed by two face-down ordinary cards).

3 Using the technique described and illustrated in The four aces (see page 100), flip the Jacks onto the pack so that the top of the pack now consists of Jack, two ordinary cards, Jack, Jack, Jack.

4 Resume your story of the burglars.

5 'Now we have all four burglars together in the garden. Remember that also in the garden, coming up the drive, was a policeman. Hearing the lookout burglar whistle, he decided to use his police whistle to summon assistance, so the four burglars decided to split up and go their various ways. They arranged to meet at ten o'clock in a favourite spot of theirs in a seedy part of town, an establishment called Barney's Bar, where knaves of all kinds liked to get together. So one burglar went south, which is always at the bottom of the map.' Take a card from the top of the pack and place it on the bottom. This card *is* a Jack, but I think it's best not to show it to the audience at this stage – they might want to see the next two.

6 'The second burglar went east.' Take the next card and place it a third of the way up the pack. 'Then the third went west.' The next card is placed a third of the way down. 'The last burglar went north, which is at the top of the map. Here he is in the northern part of town.' Lift the top card off the pack and show it to the audience. It is, of course, a Jack.

7 'So here we have a burglar in the north (show the card again), a burglar in the south (now show the audience the bottom of the pack, which does have a Jack there) and one each at east and west (point to the centre of the pack)'.

8 Now place the pack face down on the table. 'So there we have the four burglars at all four corners of the town, north, east, south and west. The police of course searched everywhere.' Pick out some of the audience and ask them to complete cuts of the cards. 'Would you Constable Charlie, please cut the cards. And you, Policewoman Lauren, Inspector Harry. Are there any other budding Inspector Morses here? What about you, Detective Sergeant William?' Encourage everybody who wants to cut the cards to do so, making sure that they complete proper cuts, and nobody tries to shuffle the pack. Proper cuts will not disturb the basic order of the cards.

9 When they have all cut the cards, pick up the pack and take a peek at the bottom card. If it's a Jack, it might be that the four Jacks are split top and bottom, which would spoil the final effect. In this case quickly put the pack back on the table, saying 'I forgot, I myself am the Chief Constable, I must have a cut.' Your cut will put the four Jacks back in the centre of the pack. But do not cut the pack yourself unless it is necessary.

10 In either case, fan through the cards face up so that the audience can see. Say 'Despite all this harrying by the forces of law and order, you will not be surprised to discover that all four of our cunning burglars got away and at the appointed time were all in a corner of their favourite bar planning their next job. Here they all are, as you can see.' Somewhere in the middle of the pack, as you fan out the cards, will be the four burglars – the four Jacks.

Push me, pull me

Skill level 3

You will need
A standard pack of cards.

Special skills
The roly-poly pass, false shuffle, double lift.

The trick
A spectator chooses and remembers a card and returns it to the centre of the pack. The pack is shuffled. The magician shows the top card of the pack to the audience and inserts it into the centre of the pack so that half of the card is sticking out. He then takes the bottom card of the pack and inserts it just below the previous card, so that is also protruding. Finally he takes another card from the bottom and inserts it just above the other two. The audience knows the identities of the three protruding cards. The spectator is then asked to take the three protruding cards between finger and thumb and push them into the pack. This pushes a group of cards out of the pack on the other side. The magician asks the spectator to push these back in again. This time a single card protrudes from the first side. The magician asks the spectator what his original chosen card was and asks him to take the protruding card from the pack. They are the same.

How to do it

1 Hand the cards to the spectator, say Oliver, and ask him to cut them. Fan them out face down, and ask him to choose a card, look at it and remember it. We'll assume it is the Jack of Spades. While he's doing this, separate the fan where the card was chosen and square up the two halves, with the bottom half in your left hand and the top half in your right. Ask Oliver to replace his card on the top of the bottom half.

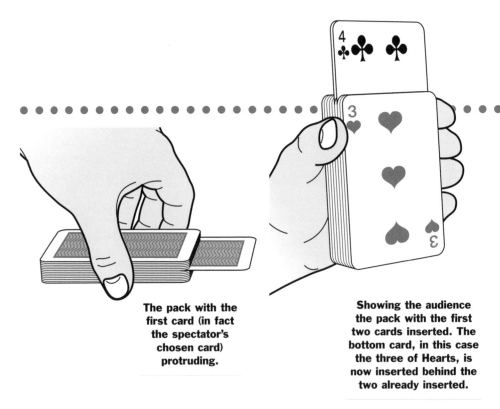

The pack with the first card (in fact the spectator's chosen card) protruding.

Showing the audience the pack with the first two cards inserted. The bottom card, in this case the three of Hearts, is now inserted behind the two already inserted.

2 Execute the roly-poly pass (see page 22) to bring the chosen card to the top of the pack, and go immediately into false shuffles 3 and 4 (see pages 12–13) to keep it there.

3 Hold the pack in your left hand and explain to your audience that, now that the cards are well shuffled, in an effort to discover Oliver's card, you are going to insert the top and bottom cards of the pack into the middle of the pack. While saying this, execute double lift 2 (see page 17). Show the audience the 'top' card, let us say the six of Diamonds (the real top card is, as we know, Oliver's chosen card).

4 Say to the audience 'The top card is the six of Diamonds.' Return the double-lifted cards to the top of the pack and take the pack with your right hand, saying 'And the bottom card is (glance at it) the four of Clubs.' Hold up the pack so that the audience can see the bottom card.

5 Now take the pack with your left hand, holding your hand palm down, so that the audience cannot see the faces of the two cards you actually place into the pack.

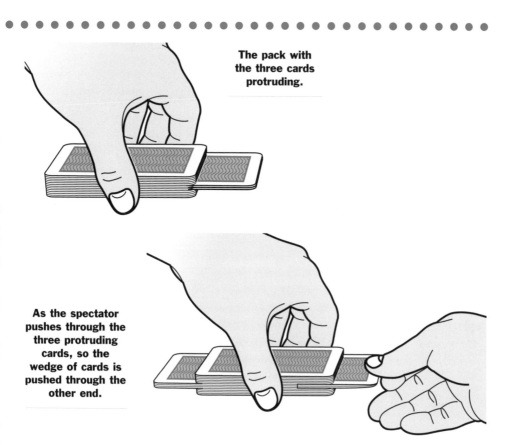

The pack with the three cards protruding.

As the spectator pushes through the three protruding cards, so the wedge of cards is pushed through the other end.

6 Take the top card from the pack and place it in the middle of the pack so that about half of it protrudes (see opposite, above left). Say 'I'll put the six of Diamonds in just there', although it is, in fact the Jack of Spades. Now take the bottom card of the pack and insert it into the pack just below (about four or five cards below) the first, saying 'I'll insert the four of Clubs just below it, there.'

7 You can now hold up the pack and show it to the audience (see opposite, above right). Point to the two protruding cards and say 'Four of Clubs and six of Diamonds. I shall now need a third card so I'll take this one at the bottom.' Let's say that one is the three of Hearts.

● ● ● ● ● ● ● ● ● ● ● ● ● ●

8 Peel off the three of Hearts, turn your left palm face down again, and insert the three of Hearts four or five cards above the top protruding card. You now have a pack that from the side looks like the top illustration on page 123. Hold it face-forward up to the audience again and pointing to the three protruding cards say 'Four of Clubs, six of Diamonds, three of Hearts.' The audience can see the four of Clubs, of course, but not the other two, the middle one of which is actually Oliver's Jack of Spades.

9 Now, while you hold the pack, ask Oliver to grasp the three protruding cards with his thumb on top and fingers below (show him how) and tell him to push the three cards back into the pack. While he does this, hold the long sides of the pack firmly and press slightly down on top with your index finger.

10 When Oliver pushes the cards into the pack a wedge of cards (about nine or ten) come through the pack at the other end (see page 123, bottom). Say to Oliver 'Now look what you've done.' Turn the pack around so that the protruding cards are facing him again. Say 'Push these back again, like you did the first three cards.'

PRACTICE

Unless you have been following this description with the cards in your hand, you may not believe that this trick works. If so, take the cards and run through it, and you will find that it does. Occasionally, if you are holding the pack too tightly or too loosely, it doesn't work very smoothly, so practise pushing the protruding cards through and back again in private until you are sure that you can work the trick smoothly each time. It is a more impressive trick than its simple operation suggests. Once you've mastered it perhaps you can invent some patter to make it seem more elaborate.

11 When Oliver does this, just one card will this time protrude at the other end of the pack. Say to Oliver 'Look, you're improving, there's only one card poking through now. Now wouldn't it be amazing if that was the card you chose and remembered? What was that card, by the way?' Oliver tells you it was the Jack of Spades. Ask him to take the protruding card from the pack and look at it and it is, of course, the Jack of Spades.

Sharing a glass

● ●

Skill level 5

You will need
A prepared pack with a double-sided card, a tumbler, a large clean handkerchief.

Special skills
False shuffle, double-turnover force, roly-poly pass, palming.

The trick
A member of the audience chooses a card at random and so does the magician. Everybody knows the magician's card because he places it in a tumbler and drapes a handkerchief over it. The spectator's card is known only to the audience, and is buried in a shuffled pack, which the magician places face down on the table. The magician says he will make the two cards change places, then reveals the card in the tumbler, which is not the card that was placed in there and the spectator confirms it is actually the card he has just picked out of the pack. He is asked to search through the pack, but his card isn't there and a further search reveals that the card which was placed in the tumbler is back in the pack. The two have mysteriously changed places.

● ●

How to do it
This trick requires a double-faced card. These can be obtained from magic shops, but it is possible to make your own (see page 129). It is also important that the backs of the cards in both packs have a white border round the pattern. This is so that if the cards get slightly out of alignment, the double-faced card is not obvious.

Let us say for the purpose of this trick you have made a double-faced card with the six of Spades on one side and the seven of Diamonds on the other.

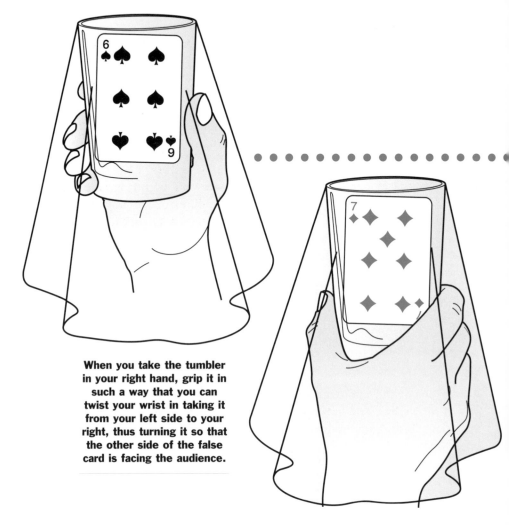

When you take the tumbler in your right hand, grip it in such a way that you can twist your wrist in taking it from your left side to your right, thus turning it so that the other side of the false card is facing the audience.

1 Arrange the pack so that the *real* six of Spades (I will refer to the double-sided card as the fake card) is at the top of the face-down pack. Make the fourth card down the fake card, with the seven of Diamonds side facing the same way as the rest of the pack. Place the *real* seven of Diamonds as the second-bottom card of the pack. This obviously means that you have 53 cards in the pack.

2 As you take the pack out of the box, place the cards face down in your left hand. Undercut the bottom half

of the pack with your right hand and take it over the top as if shuffling. However, as you drop it into your left hand take the other half of the pack in your right hand and take that over the top too, restoring the pack to its original prepared order. Do not say to the audience that you are shuffling, but do it absent-mindedly – twice if you like. The idea is to discourage any spectator from wondering if the pack is fixed.

3 Say to the audience 'For this little experiment we both have to choose a card. Yours will remain known only to

OBSERVATION

You cannot perform this trick if the audience is going to get round to either side of you or if somebody is likely to appear behind you. Make sure that everybody, even Jason and Lucy, keeps their distance, as if you were performing on a stage.

you, but as I'm a kind person I am going to let everybody see my card.'

4 Place the pack on the table and ask a volunteer to cut it by removing a few cards, say about a third of the pack. Let's call this volunteer Jason. Tell him to put his cards face up on top of the pack. Now ask another volunteer, say Lucy, to cut the pack again, taking more cards than Jason, say about half the pack. When she has done this tell her to turn her cards over and place them on top of the pack.

5 Pick the pack up and thumb off the face-up cards till you come to the first face-down card. Do this very carefully because the fourth face-down card is actually the fake card, and you mustn't let anybody see there is a face-up card mixed among the face-down ones. With the face-up cards in your left hand, push the top face-down card off from the top of the pack with your thumb and ask Jason to take it and place it face down on the table. The purpose of pushing it forward is to make it easy for Jason, who might be clumsy, to take it without disturbing the top few cards, which would reveal the fake card.

6 Say 'So you and Lucy have chosen that card. You can look at it in a moment. First of all I have to choose a

card.' Put the face-up cards that you were holding face down on top of the pack. This whole series of manoeuvres rather neatly gets the fake card nearer the centre of the pack.

7 Hold the cards up with their backs towards you and fan them out so that the audience can see their faces. Of course, somewhere in the pack one of the 'backs' of cards facing you is a fake six of Spades. Take this out and hold it up to the audience, saying 'I will have this one.' Without looking at the reverse side, lay it straight on the table, six of Spades side down. Be very careful that the audience does not get a glimpse of the underside. Looking at the card, say 'I have chosen the seven of Diamonds.'

8 Place the pack on the table and say 'Before we deal with your card, Jason, I am going to place this one in the tumbler.' Take the tumbler and hold it up in your left hand. Pick up the fake seven of Diamonds with your right hand and place it in the tumbler so that it is

More advanced magic

127

standing up for the audience to see. Be careful again not to show the reverse side to the audience. As *you* look at the card in the tumbler, it is, of course, the six of Spades.

9 With your right hand pick up the handkerchief and cover the tumbler. Taking your right hand away, reach under the handkerchief in order to take the glass from your left hand and set it on the table. As you take the tumbler twist your right wrist by 180 degrees so that you set it on the table with the six of Spades facing the audience (see page 126, top left). Practise this – you will see it can be done quite naturally without arousing any suspicion.

10 While you perform the above, tell the audience what you are doing, and as you set the tumbler down say 'Now there's the tumbler containing my card, the seven of Diamonds. We'll leave that for a minute while we deal with Jason's card, which, incidentally, none of us know at the moment. You must not let me see it Jason, so perhaps you will pick it up and show it to the audience without letting me know what it is.'

11 You know what it is anyway, of course. While Jason is showing it around, pick up the pack and divide it into two, half in each hand, ready to perform the roly-poly pass (see page 22). When Jason has shown the card

around ask him to place it on the pile in your left hand, execute the roly-poly pass and continue straight into false shuffle 1, or, if you prefer, alternate false shuffles 3 and 4 (see pages 12–13). In either case, end by retaining the six of Spades at the top.

12 Then say 'Now comes the tricky bit. I will tell you what I am about to do, and you will not believe it.' While you have the eye of the audience, palm the six of Spades from the top of the pack (see page 19). Dropping your right hand containing the six of Spades to your side, continue 'In the tumbler is the seven of Diamonds, taken at random from a fanned-out pack. In the pack here' (place the pack face down on the table) 'is a card which Jason and Lucy chose by each of them cutting a shuffled pack. You know what it is, but I don't. Believe it or not, I am going to make the two cards change places.'

13 As you are saying this, casually put your hand in your pocket and deposit the six of Spades you are holding. Now tap the top of the pack on the table with your fingers, saying 'Now, you behave yourself Jason's card, whatever you are.' Touch the top of the handkerchief with your fingers and say 'And you, seven of Diamonds, don't let me down.'

More advanced magic

14 Then, with a flourish (but also with care – you don't want to upset the tumbler) remove the handkerchief. The six of Spades is revealed. Peer round the tumbler to look at it. Say 'So, the six of Spades. I hope that was your card, Jason?' Jason agrees that indeed it was.

15 Say to him 'Do you believe that it has left that pack there' (pointing to the pack on the table) 'and flown into the glass? Perhaps you think there's another six of Spades in the pack? Would you flick through it to see, please?' Jason flicks through the pack and admits that the six of Spades has vanished.

16 Say 'Now, everybody saw me put the seven of Diamonds in the tumbler. Could you confirm that the seven of Diamonds has flown back into the pack, please?' Jason flicks through and finds the seven of Diamonds. Say 'There you are – the six of Spades and seven of Diamonds, two cards picked at random, really did change places. That's magic!'

17 Take the cards from Jason face up, put the false six of Spades on top (careful again!), turn the whole lot face down and put them in the box. Later on you can rescue the real six of Spades from your pocket and regularize the pack.

MAKING DOUBLE-FACED CARDS

You will obviously need to buy a second pack of cards from which to make false cards – make sure the second pack is of the same design as the main pack.

1 Fill a bowl with clean water, float the cards to be separated on the surface of the water and leave them overnight. Each card should separate into two halves.

2 Lay the halves flat on a clean towel to dry. Do not attempt to speed the process up with a hairdryer or anything else, because this will make the cards wrinkle or curl up.

3 When the halves are quite dry they can be carefully glued together as you wish.

4 If the cards have lost their gloss while being soaked, dab a little wax polish on the surface, and polish it with a soft cloth.

More advanced magic

Odds
and
ends

Here are a few very simple tricks you can
perform at odd times to a small audience – in
some an audience of one will do! They are
ideal for baffling people for a few minutes, but
do not repeat them as an observant person
will be able to work them out quite quickly.

Naming a card

● ●

Skill level 1

You will need
A standard pack.

The trick
A spectator places a chosen card on the pack and a certain number of cards on top of it. The magician turns his back while the spectator reads out the identities of the cards from the top of the pack. After he has read out about ten, the magician tells him which one was his chosen card.

● ●

How to do it

1 Hand the pack to a spectator, ask him to shuffle them, fan them out and remove any card he likes with a rank between one and nine. He is not to let you see it.

2 Ask him to place the pack face down on the table with his chosen card face down on top. Then turn away and tell him to count out onto the table a number of cards from the bottom of the pack corresponding to the number of the card he chose, but quietly so you can't hear him. For instance, if he chose the five of Spades, he must count out five cards from the bottom of the pack. Ask him now to place these cards face down on top of the pack. You do not know how many cards he moved from bottom to top.

3 While you are still turned away from him, ask him to turn over onto the table cards from the top of the pack and call out as he does so what cards they are.

4 All you do is, after ignoring the first card, count in your head (i.e. one, two, three) each card he calls out. You will find that one of the cards he calls out corresponds in value to the number you are counting. This is his chosen card. Do not reveal it to him immediately, but allow him to continue to ten.

Occasionally, but not often, there will be two cards that correspond, and you will have to choose one of them. If wrong, apologize and name the other one. Say you were just testing he was doing it correctly.

All done by numbers

Skill level 1

You will need
A standard pack, pen, paper and envelope.

The trick
A member of the audience shuffles the pack and deals about 15 cards to a pile on the table. While she is doing this, the magician writes a prediction on a piece of paper and places it in an envelope. Another spectator chooses a number, writes it down on a piece of paper and does a simple sum connected with it, arriving at another number. The pile of cards is counted down to that number and the corresponding card exposed. The envelope is opened, and the magician is found to have predicted the card.

How to do it

1 Hand the pack to an onlooker (let's call her Alexandra) and ask her to shuffle the cards thoroughly and begin dealing them face up into a pile on the table. While she is doing it, you begin writing on a piece of paper 'You will pick the three of Spades.' You do not complete your prediction until Alexandra has dealt the ninth card, so count carefully while Alexandra deals. The ninth card is the one you write on your prediction. Place the piece of paper in an envelope and seal it and tell Alexandra she must now stop dealing and can turn over the pile she has dealt so that it is face down. You, of course, know that the ninth card down is the one you have predicted, in this particular case, the three of Spades.

● ● ● ● ● ● ● ● ● ● ● ● ● ● ●

2 Now pass the pen and another piece of paper to another onlooker, one who you know is good at simple subtraction. Let's call him Liam. Say to him 'Now without letting me see what you are doing, write down any three-figure number you like. Done? Now write it down backwards. OK? Unless you wrote down a palindromic number (one that reads the same backwards as forwards) you will now have two different numbers. Please subtract the smaller from the larger. How many digits are there in your answer?'

3 There will be almost certainly three. Say 'Right, we'll take the middle one, which is...' The answer will be nine (it is the only possible answer – try it). Say to Alexandra 'Please count eight cards from the top of the pile and turn over the ninth.' Alexandra does so – as we know in this case it is the three of Spades. Ask her to open the envelope, reminding her and the rest as she does so that Liam chose his number at random, that she shuffled the pack herself and that you could not have known the order of the cards. Nevertheless, in your envelope is the correct prediction.

Sucker!

Skill level 1

You will need
A standard pack.

Special skill
Peeking.

The trick
An onlooker chooses a card from a fanned-out pack and replaces it. The magician and the onlooker cut the cards several times and the magician turns the cards one at a time and eventually reveals the chosen card – but there is a twist in the tail to catch out the unwary!

How to do it

1 Hand the pack to a friend and ask him to shuffle it. Let's call him Tim.

2 Take the pack back in such a way that you get a peek (see page 18) at the bottom card.

3 Fan out the pack and ask Tim to pick a card, look at it and remember what it is. While he is doing this make the pack whole and ask Tim to return his card face down to the top of the pack.

4 Complete a cut of the cards that buries Tim's card in the middle of the pack (but immediately below the card you peeked at). Ask Tim to cut the pack as well. Ask anybody else, if there are others in the party, to cut too. However many times the pack is cut, Tim's card remains below your marker card. Now tell Tim you will find his card for him.

5 With the face-down pack in your left hand, begin turning the cards over to the table one at a time. As soon as your marker card appears you know Tim's is the next. However, do not interrupt your dealing – go past Tim's card for another half-dozen cards or so.

6 Then, suddenly pause with the next card in your hand as if you know that it is Tim's. Say to him 'I bet you a fiver that the next card I turn over is yours.' Having seen his card pass by, Tim will probably jump at the offer. What you do then, of course, is put the card in your hand back on the pack and go back to Tim's card, turning it face down, much to his dismay and general amusement.

The great comedian, W.C. Fields, once wrote a book called *Never Give a Sucker an Even Break*, and would have approved of this trick which, like the Three-card Monte, was used by swindlers in the old days to separate a sucker from his cash. Of course, you wouldn't dream of taking Tim's cash.

The disappearing Ace

Skill level 1

You will need
A standard pack.

The trick
The audience is shown three Aces, fanned out. The Ace of Diamonds is between the two black Aces. The magician places the three Aces in the pack, and makes the Ace of Diamonds disappear.

How to do it
This simple trick has been around for years – it appeared in a book of card tricks written by a well-known magician of his day, L. Widdop, in 1914, and was no doubt very old by then.

1 Beforehand, you need to remove the Ace of Diamonds from the pack and hide it somewhere. Flick through the pack and lay the Aces of Spades, Hearts and Clubs face down on the table. Say to your friends 'I am now going to amaze you with a disappearing act. I am going to make a card vanish completely.' As you are saying this you put the pack face down on the table, and pick up the three cards, arranging them in a fan, which you show to your audience. Arrange them as in the illustration on the next page, so that the middle Ace appears to be the Ace of Diamonds. It is, of course, the Ace of Hearts. Say 'Here are three Aces – the Ace of Clubs, Ace of Diamonds and Ace of Spades.'

2 Before anybody can interrupt, square up the three cards and say 'Look, I'll put this one, the Ace of

How the Aces of Spades, Diamonds and Clubs are shown to the audience. The centre Ace is in reality the Ace of Hearts, pretending to be the Ace of Diamonds.

Spades, near the bottom of the pack.' Insert the Ace of Spades face down in the pack as described. While doing this, allow the audience to see that it *is* the Ace of Spades, but do not make a point of actually showing it to them, as they will expect it with the next card, too, which you cannot allow. Say 'This one (pretend to check which Ace it is by looking at it yourself, without letting the audience see it, of course), the Ace of Diamonds, I'll place in the centre of the pack.' Do so, and then, again apparently checking it, say 'I'll put this one, the Ace of Clubs, near the top of the pack.' There is no need to let the audience see this one, even though it *is* the Ace of Clubs – they saw the first Ace and will believe you about the other two.

3 Now say 'Now, what was the Ace I placed in the middle – the Ace of Diamonds wasn't it? I'll make it disappear.' Say 'Disappear!' sharply and authoritatively, at the same time 'clicking' the cards. Hold the lower half of the pack firmly between the thumb and fingers of your left hand and push the right thumb into the centre of the pack. The right fingers bend most of the top part of the pack backwards and then allow the cards to spring back one by one to the pack, making a sharp crackling noise.

4 Hand the cards back to a friend and say 'Please run through the pack to check if the Ace of Diamonds is still there. No, of course it isn't, there it is in my pocket.' Produce the card or, if you have mastered palming (see page 19), make it appear from somewhere.

Personal magnetism

●●●●●●●●●●●●●●●●●●●●●●●●●●●●●●●●●●●●●●

Skill level 1

You will need
A standard pack.

The trick
The magician and an onlooker take half of a shuffled pack each. The magician turns his back while the onlooker selects a card from her half-pack, remembers it, and places it face down on top of her half. The magician turns round and places his half-pack on top of that. The onlooker now takes the whole pack behind her back and moves three cards as instructed, including turning one over and inserting it in the pack. On examination, the turned-over card is found to be next to the card that the onlooker originally chose.

●●●●●●●●●●●●●●●●●●●●●●●●●●●●●●●●●●●●●●

How to do it

1 A spectator, let's call her Alice, shuffles the pack. Ask her to divide the pack into two halves and hand one half to you. Say 'I'm going to turn my back, Alice, while you select any card, remember it, and place it on top of the pack.'

2 While your back is turned you make slight adjustments to your half of the pack. Turn two cards face up: the second one from the top and the bottom one. Ask Alice if she has finished her part, and if so turn around. Ask her what she did. This is to make sure that she followed instructions and that her chosen card is the top card on her pack. Ask her to put it on the table and place your pack on top of it.

3 Ask Alice to take the whole pack behind her back and face the audience, since you do not wish anyone to see her manipulations with the cards (they will notice one of the cards that you have turned face up).

4 Tell Alice 'You have to move three cards, Alice. Take the top card and place it somewhere near the bottom of the pack. OK? Now take the bottom card and place it somewhere near the top. Right? Now take the new top card and turn it over. Now place it near the centre of the pack. OK? Fine. Now you can give me the pack back.'

5 Take the pack from Alice and explain what you hope to achieve. Say 'What I'm hoping, Alice, and this rarely fails, is that you have found the original card you chose with the one you inserted face up in the pack. I don't know how this works, but I believe it's all to do with your personal magnetism. The card you've turned over automatically by instinct seeks out the one you chose a little earlier.'

6 Fan out the cards face down so that all can see, and near the middle will be a face-up card (not, of course, the one Alice turned over – she merely put right one of the cards you had turned over).

7 Say 'Ah, here's the card you turned over, and the one below it should be your original choice. Tell us, what was your original card?' Alice names it. Ask her to take out and announce the card below the face-up card. It will be the card of her choice.

Envelope prediction

You will need
One standard pack, an envelope,
pen and paper.

Special skills
Peeking.

The trick
A spectator shuffles the pack, then
chooses any 12 cards, handing the
rest back to the magician. The
spectator reshuffles her 12 while
the magician writes a prediction on
a piece of paper which he places in
an envelope and puts to one side.
The spectator lays any four of her
cards face up on the table in a line
and hands the rest back to the
magician. The magician adds cards
from the pack face down onto each
card on the table to bring its value
to ten, e.g. if the card were a
three, he would add seven cards to
it. For this purpose court cards
count as ten, and require no added
cards. The pip values of the four
exposed cards are now added
together (court cards again
counting ten) and the magician
counts off that number of cards
from the remainder of the pack.
The last dealt he turns over. The
envelope is opened to find the
magician has predicted the
exposed card.

How to do it

1 A member of the audience, let's call her Annie, shuffles. She is asked to take any 12 cards and reshuffle them. When she hands the remainder back to you, you take a peek at the bottom card. Let us say it is the seven of Clubs. You write the name of this card on the piece of paper and put it in the envelope, sealing it and setting it on the table.

2 Ask Annie to lay any four of her cards face up on the table and give the rest to you, which you add to the bottom of your pile. You then deal cards onto each of Annie's face-up cards bringing the value of each pile up to ten (court cards count as ten), as described above. You then ask Annie to add up the values of the four cards she laid on the table. Check that she's adding them up correctly.

3 Count out cards from your hand down to the corresponding number and reveal the seven of Clubs, which is, of course, the card you predicted.

EXPLANATION

This is an arithmetical trick which cannot fail (unless there is a miscount, or a card missing!). When you took eight back from Annie and put them on the bottom of the pack the seven of Clubs became the ninth card from the bottom, or the fortieth from the top, there being four cards on the table.

Now suppose the values of the four cards on the table are 18. The number of cards you need to add to them to bring each pile up to ten will be 22. There will now be 26 cards left in your hand, and the eighteenth card down will be the seven of Clubs.

In other words the values of the four upturned cards, together with the number of cards needed to be added to them, will always be 40, and the fortieth card in the pack is the one you peeked at and wrote down.

Copy me

Skill level 1

You will need
Two packs of cards, preferably with different designs on the back.

Special skill
Peeking.

The trick
The magician and a spectator have a pack of cards each, which they shuffle. They exchange packs to shuffle each other's, and return them. Each selects a card at random, returns it to the pack, and the cards are cut. They exchange packs and each removes the card they selected. The two cards prove to be identical.

How to do it

1 Choose a member of the audience to be your partner. Let's call her Molly. Hand her one of the packs and ask her to check that it is a regular standard pack. Say to her 'In this experiment, you must do with your cards exactly what I do with mine. At the end we might find that we come to a surprising result. First of all, we'll both give our cards a good shuffle.'

2 When done, say 'Now we'll exchange packs and shuffle each other's. Before you shuffle mine, you can fan through to make sure that my pack, too, is a standard regular pack. OK? No tricks there? Good.'

3 When you have shuffled Molly's pack, square it up, taking a quick peek at the bottom card. Let's assume it's the eight of Hearts.

4 Place Molly's pack face down in front of her and ask her to do the same with yours. Say 'Now, take out a card from anywhere within the pack, look at it and remember it. I will do the same. Then we will each put our chosen cards back on top of the pack.' In fact, although you go through this procedure, there is no need for you to remember what your card is at all.

5 When this is done say 'Now we each cut our packs, like this.' In case Molly is not aware of how to complete a cut, show her with your pack by taking about half the cards from the top, placing them on the table and putting the remaining half on top.

6 Say 'Good. Now we exchange packs again. Now you look through my pack for the card you chose and lay it face down on the table. I will look through your pack and do the same.'

7 All you do, of course, is look for the eight of Hearts in Molly's pack. The one above it, or to the right of it, as you fan out the cards will be the card that Molly selected. You take this out and lay it face down on the table.

8 Say 'Molly, what would you say the chances are that we both picked the same card? I'll tell you. Precisely 51 to 1. But if my little experiment is a success that's what we will have done. Let's turn over our cards and see.'

9 You both turn over your cards and they are revealed to be identical.

Found at last

You will need
A standard pack.

The trick
A spectator chooses a card and returns it to the pack. The magician deals the pack into two piles, one face up, one face down, and asks the spectator to stop him as soon as the chosen card appears face up. When it doesn't, the magician repeats the operation with the face-down cards. The spectator's card is, remarkably, the last one to appear.

How to do it

1 Shuffle the pack, fan it out, and ask the spectator, let's say Mark, to choose a card, look at it and remember it. As you fan out the cards, count out 21 from the right and make a slight gap between the twenty-first and twenty-second cards. It is not difficult to count out the 21 – the best way is to count in threes. But place accuracy before speed, because 20 or 22 is no good – the trick will not work.

2 When Mark has taken his card, separate the 21 from the rest because you want Mark to replace his card on the pile in your left hand, so that when you cover it with the pile in your right hand, Mark's card is the twenty-second. Of course, having slightly separated your 21 cards, if Mark chooses one of them, you must slide another card across to your right hand. It is not a good idea to leave the counting of the 21 cards until Mark has taken his

card, as it becomes a little obvious that you are counting, and very obvious if Mark tries to return his card while you are still in the process of counting.

3 With Mark's card safely in the twenty-second place, begin dealing two piles, the first face up, the second face down, telling Mark to stop you when his card appears face up. It won't.

4 Pick up the face-down pack and repeat the operation. Again Mark's card will not appear. Start to express surprise as Mark's card does not show as deals go by. In fact, it will still not have appeared when there are three cards left. Two more will be dealt face up – neither of them Mark's. Say to Mark 'Are you sure you've been watching? Surely your card cannot be the very last one?' Turn over the only card left in your hand, and it's Mark's. Say 'Well, that's remarkable. Would you believe it?'

Odds and ends

Indian magic

You will need
A standard pack.

The trick
A spectator shuffles and, while the magician's back is turned, deals two equal piles of as many cards as he likes. He hands one pile to another spectator and each cuts his pile, looks at the card he cuts at, and returns the top half of his pack to the other spectator's bottom half. The two packs are then joined in whatever order the spectators choose, and cut as many times as they wish. The magician sees none of this, but with his own special shuffle of the cards brings the two cards chosen by the spectators together.

How to do it
This trick is chosen for its somewhat unique ending and its effect depends a lot on the patter.

1 Hand the pack to an onlooker, say George, and turn your back. Ask George to shuffle the pack and then deal two equal face-down piles to the table of as many cards as he wishes. Suggest between eight and fifteen in each pile to keep the trick to manageable proportions. Tell him to put the unused cards aside. Ask him to place one pile face down in front of himself and the other in front of another onlooker, say Kenny.

2 Say to George and Kenny 'Please both cut your piles by taking a few cards off the top. Now look at the bottom card of the pile in your hand, and remember it, but place the cards back on each other's piles – in other words, George, place your cards on Kenny's pile, and, Kenny, place yours on George's. OK? Now, you've now got two piles before you. Place one pile on top of the other. It doesn't matter which goes on top. Done? Good.'

3 You can now turn round, where there will be one pile of cards on the table (not counting those discarded). Ask Kenny and George to make a complete cut of the cards again.

4 Now pick up the pack and say 'Each of you has chosen a card at random from a shuffled pack and buried the cards in this pack, which has been subsequently cut twice. The two cards

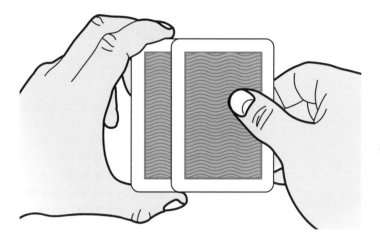

can be anywhere. I have no idea what either card is. However, using an ancient Indian shuffle, I am going to try to bring those two cards together. Watch this. Nothing up my sleeves.'

5 With the cards held in your left hand, thumb at the rear short side and fingers at the other, use your right thumb and fingers to pull off the top and bottom cards of the pack together (see above). Place these face down on the table, and continue in the same manner until you have dealt each pair to the pile on the table (note: if you have a card over in your left hand you have misdealt, or George did not deal two equal piles. In this case it's best to point out there's been a misdeal and start again, emphasizing each step as you go).

6 Now turn the cards over and begin doing the same thing with the cards face up, telling George and Kenny to stop you as soon as they see either of their cards. Take care while you're doing this not to let anybody see the bottom card of the pair you are dealing.

7 As soon as either Kenny or George recognizes his card deal that pair to one side and place the rest of the cards with those already dealt.

8 Say 'If the ancient magician who taught me this shuffle is correct, then the card that is under George's card is Kenny's card. Personally I never know whether to believe it or not. What was your card Kenny?' Kenny names his card, you lift up George's card, and below it is Kenny's.

OBSERVATION

This is a mathematical trick that cannot fail, so if the card you expose is a wrong card, there is a misdeal somewhere. Say 'I've never known the magician wrong before. I think somewhere somebody has misdealt. Shall we try it again?'

The Q-trick

You will need
A standard pack and a pencil and paper.

The trick
The cards are given to a spectator, who is asked to shuffle them and lay them out face up on the table in the form of a capital letter Q (see page 148). The number of cards in the tail of the Q is left to his choice. The magician writes a prediction on a piece of paper. The spectator is asked to count out loud the cards in the Q, starting from the end of the tail and proceeding clockwise up the left-hand side, touching each of the cards with his finger as he goes. He is told he can stop when he likes. He is then asked to count back similarly anti-clockwise, starting on the card he stopped on, but missing out the tail of the Q. He is to stop when he reaches the same number as before. The magician then shows the piece of paper, on which he has written the name of the card at which the spectator finished.

How to do it
This is a simple trick which works itself, and is obvious if you think about it. The number of cards in the tail of the Q equals the number of cards that the spectator (let's call him Matt) reaches up the right-hand side of the Q when he counts back. Thus all you have to do when the cards are laid out is secretly to count the number of cards in the tail, count the same number up the right-hand side of the Q and predict the card you come to as the one which Matt will stop on. Obviously it doesn't matter how many cards Matt counts before he stops, he will end on that card when he counts back. Be certain, though, that the card he stops on he counts as 'one' when he counts back.

Odds and ends

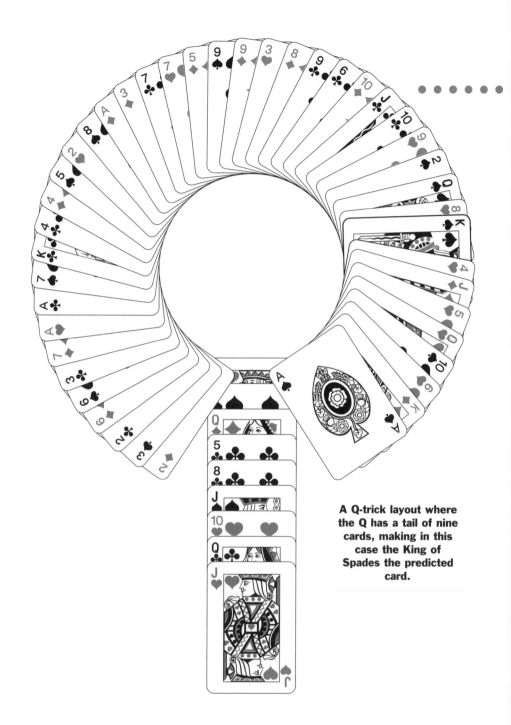

A Q-trick layout where the Q has a tail of nine cards, making in this case the King of Spades the predicted card.

The trick cannot be repeated, and you shouldn't give the audience any time to think about it before you move on to the next.

Improved versions

This trick would obviously be more impressive if the cards were laid face down rather than face up. This can be done, if the pack is prepared beforehand and the cards aren't shuffled. Two ways of doing this are suggested: one is very simple, the other just simple.

The very simple way is to deal out the cards into the Q yourself. Make the tail, say, nine cards long and have the pack arranged so that you know the identity of the ninth card from the bottom of the pack. Say to Matt 'What I want you to do is to count out loud from the foot of the tail here and around the left-hand side here, touching each card as you go and stopping wherever you like. Leave your finger on the card at which you stop. Before you start I am going to predict, by writing on this piece of paper, the card at which you will eventually stop.'

The slightly more difficult way is to allow Matt to deal the cards as before, and to let him put as many as he likes (up to ten, say) in the tail of the Q (but do not let him shuffle them). This means that you must arrange and memorize the bottom ten cards of the pack. If you have already learned the order of the 'eight-King-three' pre-arranged pack (see page 76), then make the bottom ten cards of the pack the first ten in that

(see page 76)

system. If not, make them something simple you can remember, e.g. two, four six, eight, ten, Ace, three, five, seven, nine of, alternately, Clubs, Hearts, Spades, Diamonds. Once Matt has laid down the tail of his Q, you will have plenty of time to run through in your mind the card he will end on. For instance, if he makes a tail of seven, in the pack prepared under the 'eight-King-three' system, he will end on the nine of Spades, while on the pack prepared under the suggested quick system, he will end on the three of Spades.

Odds and ends

Upside down trick

Skill level 1

You will need
Four fives and four Kings from a standard pack.

The trick
The magician takes the four fives from a standard pack of cards and lays them in a row. He turns his back and any number of the cards are turned through 180 degrees by members of the audience. The magician then points out which cards have been turned. If someone in the audience points out that only the three of Diamonds is symmetrical, the magician repeats the trick using the four Kings.

How to do it
This is hardly a trick at all, merely exploiting a fact about playing cards that few people know. It arises from the difficulty in the printing and trimming of cards to get the image exactly in the centre of the card, even with sophisticated modern manufacturing methods.

1 Examine the fives from a standard pack. The five is chosen because the figure five has a horizontal bar at the top that runs parallel with the edge of the card. Compare the space between the bar and the edge of the card at one end with that at the other. It is likely that there is a difference, which might be less than 1mm (½₀in) but which is nevertheless quite easily spotted with the naked eye. And this will probably apply to all four fives. If this is true of your pack, you can perform this trick.

2 Take the four fives from the pack and lay them in a row (see above). Say to a member of the audience, let's say Dave 'In a moment, Dave, I will turn my back, or even leave the room if you like. When I do so, I want you to turn any number of these cards through 180 degrees, like this.' Under the pretext of

showing Dave what is wanted, turn whichever card or cards is necessary to make all four have the narrow gap between number and edge at the top (i.e. the end farthest from you).

3 Turn your back, or leave the room if the audience insist, so that Dave can do as you asked. When you turn back, look closely at the cards and you will be able to see at a glance which have been turned.

4 You may repeat this trick as often as you wish, and allow the cards to be examined, without much chance of anybody working out how it's done.

5 Of course, if you do repeat the trick, you must repeat it with the cards as they lie – it would be a giveaway if you turned the cards back to their original

Odds and ends

151

● ● ● ● ● ● ● ● ● ● ● ● ● ● ● ●

positions. So you must remember which cards have the narrow space at the top and which at the bottom after each trick. In practice of course all you need to remember is something like: 'Spades and Diamonds top'. You can then tell which cards have been turned even if the audience try to fool you by moving their positions in the row.

6 Now look at the illustration (page 151). Does anything strike you about the fives? If you eliminate the five of diamonds, you could perform this trick in a much simpler way, by virtue of the fives of Spades, Clubs and Hearts not being symmetrical, because of the suit symbol in the centre. The Heart, for instance, could be either pointing up or down. Let us hope somebody in the audience will spot this and announce it.

7 'Very good,' you say. 'You are clearly a very clever audience and not to be easily fooled. In actual fact very few cards are symmetrical – even the sixes and eights have these pips in the centre which point in one way.' Flick through the pack and show the audience a six and an eight (not of Diamonds) to show them what you mean.

NOTE

It is unnecessary, I hope, to point out that you should check that the pack you are going to use for this trick does have this slightly off-centre printing of the fives and kings. Before performing before an audience, practise to make certain that you can spot without fail which way up the cards are.

8 Then with a thoughtful look say 'Of course the picture cards are absolutely symmetrical. I don't suppose I could do the trick with them. Let's see how it works with the Kings.'

9 Take out the four Kings (there is a good straight edge at the top of the 'K' to make the gap between it and the edge of the card easily measured) and lay them out in a row. Note which suits have the narrow gap at the top. Repeat the trick with the Kings and leave your audience baffled.

Right second attempt

You will need
A standard pack.

Special skills
Roly-poly pass, false shuffle.

The trick
A spectator chooses a card from a shuffled pack, remembers it and replaces it. The magician shuffles again, divides the pack into two, the audience member choosing half, the magician having the other. Each deals from his pile a number of cards decided upon by the spectator. Each turns over the top card of the new pile. Neither card matches the helper's chosen card. They swap piles and repeat the exercise. This time one of them turns up the chosen card.

How to do it
Hand the pack to a member of the audience (let's call him Mark) and ask him to shuffle the cards thoroughly. Taking back the pack make a face-down fan of it and ask him to choose a card, examine it, remember it and replace it on the half of the pack in your left hand. With the half of the pack in your right hand perform the roly-poly pass (see page 22), which places the chosen card on top of the pack, and go straight into false shuffle 1 or successive false shuffles 2 and 3 (see page 12) to keep the chosen card on top of the pack.

1 Then divide the pack in two placing the two halves on the table. Say to Mark: 'Which of the two piles do you suppose contains your chosen card?' Ask him to pick it up while you take the other one.

2 Now ask him to guess how many cards down in the pile his card might be. Suppose he says the tenth card. Say 'OK, we'll both deal face down onto the table ten cards.' When you have done this ask Mark to turn over the top card of the pile he has dealt to the table to see if it is his card. It isn't. (In fact his card is at the bottom of one of the piles. You know which pile it is).

Odds and ends

153

3 Turn over the top card of your pack. This isn't the chosen card either. Say 'This is what we'll do. We'll each put the card we looked at back on our pile and then put that pile back onto the pile in our hands. Now we'll swap piles and see if we have better luck.'

4 Exchange piles and say 'Now I'll deal ten cards face down onto the table from this pile and you do the same from that one.'

5 When you've done this, one of the piles on the table is topped by the chosen card. You know which one it is. The trick works best if the chosen card is the last one to be exposed. And it's best, too, if Mark names the card before it's exposed.

6 Assume that the chosen card is on top of Mark's pile. Say 'Before we look at these two, what was your chosen card by the way?' Mark will name it. Let's suppose it is the two of Diamonds. Turn over your card and say 'Well I haven't got it, what about you?' Mark turns over his card – the two of Diamonds.

7 Say 'Well, it took two attempts, but we got it right in the end.'

Mix two or three

Skill level 1

You will need
The 13 cards of one suit.

The trick
The 13 cards of a suit are arranged in rank order. The magician deals them one at a time face down onto the table. At any time a spectator may stop him and say 'Mix two,' or Mix three.' In this case the magician deals two or three cards at once as directed. He picks up the cards and runs through the procedure again with a second spectator. The pack is then picked up and turned over, and instead of being well mixed is shown to be in its original order.

●●●●●●●●●●●●●●●●●●●●●●●●●●●●●●●●

How to do it

1 Take out all the cards of one suit, say Diamonds, and arrange them in order, Ace to King, and show the arrangement to the audience. Take the cards face down in your left hand and say 'I need an assistant to call some instructions. Will you help, Sally? I am going to deal the cards face down to the table one at a time. You can interrupt at any time you like by calling 'Mix two,' or 'Mix three,' when, instead of dealing one card I will deal two or three as directed. OK?'

2 Deal the cards one at a time. Say Sally calls 'Mix two,' as you are about to deal the third card. Take the third card and place it under the fourth, and deal the two cards together to the table. Suppose as you are about to deal the seventh card, Sally says 'Mix three.' Take the seventh card in between your right thumb and first two fingers, push the eighth card with your left thumb on top of it and the ninth card on top of the previous two in the same way. Drop all three on to the pile on the table, and continue.

3 Once all cards are dealt to the table, take them in your left hand again, turn to another spectator, and say: 'I'll repeat that exercise. Perhaps this time you, Don can call out the instructions.'

4 Deal the cards again to the table.

5 Pick them all up and say: 'Well, by now they should be well mixed up, but to demonstrate my mastery over the cards – watch!'

6 Take the cards in one hand and riff them, i.e. flick the cards at one end. Turn them over and say 'Look, all the cards are back in rank order. They know who's boss.'

Another prediction

You will need
A standard pack, pen and paper.

Special skills
False shuffle.

The trick
A spectator is handed the pack, asked to think of a number (which he keeps secret) and deals that number of cards onto the table. While he is doing this the magician turns his back and writes the name of a card on a piece of paper. The spectator is then asked to deal from his pile a number of cards based on the number he thought of originally. He turns over the top card of the remaining pile and the magician shows that it is the card he wrote on the piece of paper.

How to do it

1 Fan out the cards as if checking they contain no joker. While doing so, look at and remember the ninth card from the bottom of the pack (see next page). This is not exactly peeking, but it needs a little concentration to do it naturally, without making it obvious. Instead of counting one to nine, you might find it easier to count off three packets of three, the top card of the third three being the ninth card from bottom.

2 Having memorized this card (let's say it's the King of Diamonds), perform false shuffle 1 (page 11), to keep the top nine cards or more in position. Hand the pack face down to a volunteer, let's call him Jim. The King of Diamonds is the ninth card from the top.

3 Say: 'Jim, please think of a number, not too small or too big – let's say between 10 and 19. Do not tell it to me. What I'd like you to do is deal from the top of the pack one by one, face down, the number of cards corresponding to the number you thought of.'

4 Wait till Jim starts (make sure he doesn't shuffle the cards himself before he starts dealing) and then turn your back, saying 'While you're doing that I'll turn my back and write a prediction on this piece of paper.'

5 Write down the name of the card which you know is ninth from the

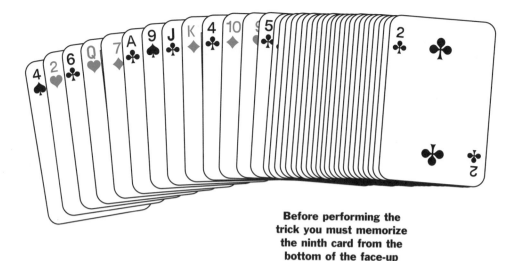

Before performing the trick you must memorize the ninth card from the bottom of the face-up pack, in this case the King of Diamonds.

top of the pack (in this case the King of Diamonds). Fold the paper in half.

6 Turn back again and say 'Have you done that, Jim? Good. Put the main pack aside and take up the cards you've just dealt. Now whatever the number was you first thought of, add together the two digits to get a new number – for instance if it was 16, add 1 and 6 to get 7. OK? Now deal to the table that number of cards from those in your hand. Right. Now let's review what you've done. You've taken a shuffled pack, thought of a number which you kept to yourself and by using that number twice in different ways you've arrived at a small pile of cards in your hand. Now there's no way anybody could know the top card of that pile, is there? It could be any one of the 52 cards, could it not? Right, will you please turn it over?' (Make sure he turns over the top card in his hand, not the top card on the table).

7 Jim turns over the card. It is the King of Diamonds. You say 'Well, that is quite remarkable. Look at what I predicted on this piece of paper.'

8 You unfold your piece of paper, on which you have written 'King of Diamonds'.

NOTE

This trick must work because if Jim deals 13 cards, he later removes 4 (1 + 3), if he deals 18, he removes 9 (1 + 8). Whichever number he chooses, the card on top in his hand will be the original ninth card from the top of the pack, which you carefully memorized and predicted.

The Jacks' backs

You will need
Four Jacks from two separate packs with different coloured backs.

The trick
A member of the audience is shown the Jacks of the four suits and asked to select one. The magician claims he can force him to choose whichever one he wishes. When the spectator has chosen his card, the magician shows him that the chosen card has a different coloured back to the other three.

How to do it
This trick relies purely on cheek. It is surprising how often you can get away with it. From one pack (in this instance they have grey backs) you take the two black Jacks, and from another pack of the same design, but with the backs of a different colour (in this instance, red) the two red Jacks. Keep these in an envelope in your pocket, as you do not use them for other tricks.

1 You show the four Jacks to the audience, taking care not to show the backs, and you say to one of them, perhaps Andy 'If I asked you to select one of these Jacks, and you picked one, you would think that you picked it of your own free choice, wouldn't you? You wouldn't think that I could force you to pick the one I wanted you to pick, would

you?' Andy would probably reply that of course you couldn't influence his choice at all.

2 Say 'All right, Andy, let's see. Please name one of these Jacks.' Andy will choose one of the four suits. Ask him if he would like to change his mind. Perhaps he will, perhaps he won't, but let's say he finally decides on the Jack of Clubs. Say 'You have chosen the Jack of Clubs, Andy, and it was your free choice, uninfluenced by me, correct?'

3 As you are saying this, rearrange the four cards, so that the Jack of Spades (i.e. the Jack of the same colour as the one Andy chose) is on top of the face-up cards. At the same time withdraw the Jack of Clubs and say 'This is your chosen card.' Show it to Andy

Odds and ends

159

Put the chosen card (in this case the Jack of Clubs) at the bottom of the pile, with the Jack of the same colour on the top. The colours of the backs of the cards are as on the right.

and the audience and replace it at the bottom of the four Jacks (see above).

4 Square up the four cards and take them in your right hand, palm up, with your four fingers along the long side nearer the audience, your thumb at the side nearest you, the cards face down. At the top of the four cards is an grey-backed card (the Jack of Clubs).

5 Show the grey back to the audience and turning your hand palm down, with the fingers of your left hand draw off the bottom card (i.e. the Jack of Clubs) into your left-hand palm, saying 'You chose the Jack of Clubs, which has an grey back.' Turning your right hand palm up again, you show the audience a red-backed card. Turning the palm face down again, draw off with your left thumb the card from the top card of the

pile so that it rests on the jack of clubs. This is of course the other grey-backed card (the Jack of Spades). As you do this, say 'The second card has a red back,' quickly turning your right-hand palm up again to show what appears to be another red back, but is in fact the same one, continue 'As does the third card.' Turn your right hand face down, draw off the bottom card with your fingers and turn over the last card to show that it, too, has a red back. Drop it onto the cards in your left palm and say 'You see, Andy, you chose the only card to have an grey back, as I forced you to do.'

6 Put the cards back into the envelope and return it to your pocket. It is best not to repeat the trick – the next onlooker might choose the 'only' jack with a red back!

Odds and ends

Royal games

● ●

Skill level 1

You will need
The King, Queen and Jack of Clubs, Hearts and Diamonds.

The trick
The nine cards above are placed in three piles face up in their suits. A member of the audience selects a suit, shuffles the cards and lays them face down in a row. She does the same in turn with the other two suits, and then collects up the three piles. She cuts them as often as she likes, deals them into two fresh piles and makes a single pack of them. By spelling out the three suits, the magician amazingly sorts the cards out into their suits again. He repeats the trick twice, the second repeat producing a surprise result.

● ●

How to do it
This is a very amusing trick that works itself, so no skill is necessary, but you must be very careful. It is easy to make a mistake.

1 Make three piles of cards, face up – with the King, Queen and Jack of Hearts, in any order in one pile, and the same ranks of Clubs and Diamonds in the two other piles (see page 162).

2 Saying 'This is a trick for the royals only,' ask a member of the audience, let's say Jessica, to choose one of the suits. Pick up the three cards, shuffle them and deal them face down in a row. Then ask her to take another suit and do the same, dealing one card on to each of the three in the row already dealt, in any order she likes. Then ask her to do the same with the third suit so that she ends with three piles of three cards, face down.

3 Now say 'Jessica, please pick up the three piles placing them one on another in any order you wish. Now place the whole pile on the table and cut it, placing the bottom half on top of the top half. Good. Would you like to cut the cards again? You can cut them as many times as you wish. Now please make two piles by dealing the cards alternately face down. Excellent. Now put whichever

**Three piles are
made of the
court cards
(Jack, Queen,
King) of any
Diamonds,
Clubs and
Hearts.**

pile you like on top of the other. Perfect.
You can cut the cards again if you like.
OK? Want to make the two piles again?
Are you satisfied? You've done a lot of
work, so you can now give the cards
back to me. Thank you. Obviously, I
cannot possibly know the order of the
nine cards in this little pile, but I'll try to
separate them back into their suits by
spelling out the names of the suits.
Let's start with a Club.'

4 Now, holding the cards face down,
spell out loud the word CLUB,
moving a card from top to bottom for the
letters C, L and U, but placing the fourth
card face down on the table as you
announce the last letter, B.

5 Say, 'Now, we'll try the Heart suit.'
(Notice you do not say 'Clubs' or
'Hearts', because if you do, the
audience might wonder why you do not
spell out the 's' on the end of the words
'Clubs' and 'Hearts').

6 You repeat the procedure, spelling
out HEART and playing the card
representing the T on the table to the
right of the card already there. Then you
spell out DIAMOND in the same way,
placing the card representing the last
letter to the right of the others, making a
face-down row of three.

7 Now say 'We'll do it again, but we'll
start at the other end of the row
this time.' You spell out CLUB, but you
put down the card representing B on top
of the card at the right-hand end of the

Odds and ends

row. This is perhaps the easiest thing to forget in this whole trick. Forget it, and the trick is sunk. Spell out HEART again (putting the card for T on the middle pile) and DIAMOND, as before, putting it on the left-hand pile. Then say: 'Well, we'll speed up the procedure now – I'll just deal these last three cards onto the piles.' Place the cards one on each pile, beginning again with the right-hand pile.

8 Now say 'Right, that's that, shall we see if I've been successful?' Turn over the three piles and one will be all Clubs, another all Hearts and the third all Diamonds.

9 If nobody asks you to perform the trick again, say 'Now we're back to three piles of cards sorted by suits, would you like to see it again? Pick up any suit you like, shuffle the cards and deal them face down in a row.'

10 Repeat the trick as before.

11 This time when the cards are in their suits, note the order of the third pile – let's say it's Jack, King, Queen. Pick up the first pile and casually arrange them in the same order – you might have to move one or two cards. Do the same with the second pile, as you add it to the first. Then pick up the

third pile, which is already in the required order, and add it to the others, saying 'I tell you what, we'll do it once more, and I'll see if I can make something different happen. Perhaps you, Becky, will help this time, and we'll speed it up a little. Just take the cards and, if you like, cut them. Do you want to cut them again? OK, now deal them into two piles as the others did. Now put either pile on top of the other. Do you want to cut them again? Right, give them back to me and let's see what happens.'

12 You then go through the usual procedure, spelling out CLUB, HEART and DIAMOND, and making three piles of face down cards.

13 Saying 'Now let's see what we've got,' turn over the three piles. One will be all Kings, one all Queens, and one all Jacks.

14 Say 'Well, the cards seem to have minds of their own, don't they? That's amazing. Who would have thought it?' Certainly not your audience, who are dumbfounded. Pick up the cards and stop there.

Look no hands

Skill level 3

You will need
A standard pack.

Special skills
The peek, false shuffle 4.

The trick
The magician shuffles and hands the pack to a spectator, who cuts it into three piles. The spectator chooses a pile, and looks at and remembers a card from that pile. The card is replaced in another pile, which the spectator deals out one at a time onto the table. The magician recognizes the chosen card from how the spectator reacts.

How to do it
As you idly shuffle the cards, take a peek (see page 18) at the bottom card. Execute false shuffle 4 (see page 13) to move this card to the top, at the same time taking a peek at the bottom card. You now know the top and bottom cards of the pack.

1 Say 'I need a volunteer to help with this trick – in fact almost to perform it, since I am going to hand the pack over and not touch it again. Who is willing to take part?' Let us say Kirsty volunteers.

2 Hand the cards to Kirsty saying 'Please cut them into three face-down piles, by dropping a section onto the table, then another, then the last. That's right.'

3 The three piles are as opposite. You know the bottom card of pile A and the top card of pile C, but nothing at all about pile B.

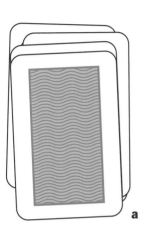 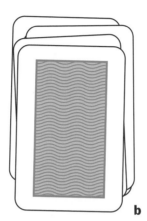 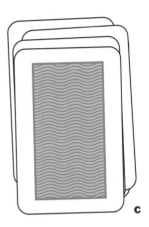

a   b   c

4 Say to Kirsty 'I now want you to choose one of these three piles by pointing at it.'

5 The routine now depends upon which pile Kirsty chooses. Let's suppose it is A. Say 'You've chosen that pile. Pick it up and look at the bottom card. Take it, remember it and place it into either of the other piles. Now thoroughly shuffle that pile so that I cannot possible know which card you chose.' Of course, in fact you already know it.

6 If Kirsty chooses pile C, ask her to take the top card, look at it, remember it, and bury it into one of the other piles, and shuffle. Once again you know the card which Kirsty chose.

7 In both of these cases you now say to Kirsty 'Now I want you to take the pile in which your card is hidden and deal the cards face up one at a time. What I am going to do is to study you closely and hope that when you deal the card which you chose you will react, so that I will be able to tell what your card is. It's a bit like submitting to a truth drug test. The idea is that you will not be able to prevent a flicker as you deal your card. I'll stop you when I think your card appears, but if I don't, don't tell me. Sometimes I need a second chance.'

8 Of course you know as soon as Kirsty lays down the card, and can stop her and reveal it. But if it's one of the first three she deals it might be best to let it pass. At the end say 'I'm sorry I missed it. It's probably because it was one of the first few, and it went before I was switched on to your reactions. Just run through the first few again and I'll hope to spot it.' When Kirsty turns over the card, say 'Ah yes – that's the one. There was a definite tremor there.'

9 If Kirsty chooses pile B, your procedure is different, because now you genuinely do not know the card. Say to her, 'Take the top card, look at it and remember it. Now place it on top of one of the other two piles.' When Kirsty has done this, say 'Now please cut that pile, and transfer the bottom half to the top.' Now tell her, in the same way as above, to deal the cards one by one. Note – you must not let her shuffle.

10 This time the chosen card will appear about half-way through, so you can identify it immediately. If Kirsty puts her card on pile A, it will appear immediately after the bottom card of the pack you peeked at before you gave it to her, so you can say 'Ah – that's the one. I sensed a little nervous reaction there, just when you dealt that card.'

WARNING

A long time and a lot of patter passes between the time you peeked at the two cards in the beginning and the time you reveal the chosen card at the end. Concentrate on not forgetting what the two cards were!

11 If Kirsty puts her card on pile C, however, when she deals them out, it will appear one before the card you peeked at, so you won't know it immediately. But as soon as she deals the next card you will know. Say 'Wait a minute, Kirsty. You seem to me a bit anxious to deal this card, as if the previous card was your chosen card.' Name it and ask 'Was that the one?' Kirsty will admit it was.

One over the eight

Skill level 1

You will need
Any nine cards (including a nine), an accomplice, and a pencil.

The trick
Nine cards are laid out in a pattern. The magician asks for a volunteer from among the audience to help and the volunteer is instructed to leave the room. Another volunteer is asked to choose one of the nine cards by pointing to it. The person who left the room is asked to return, and indicates which of the nine cards was chosen.

How to do it
This is a trick I first learnt as a child some 60 years ago. It is simplicity itself and it is surprising how many times you can perform it without the audience spotting how it is done. Of course, if you have performed a few tricks already, and many of your audience have genuinely assisted at picking a card, etc, there is no reason at first for them to suspect that the assistant for this trick is actually an accomplice. But even when they do suspect, as they will eventually, it is still another step to working out how you do it.

1 Casually fiddle with the cards before you begin. All you have to do is make sure that a nine of any suit is among the top nine cards.

2 Begin by saying 'For this next effect, I need any nine cards, so I'll just take the top nine from the pack.'

3 Count out nine cards face down onto the table. Your accomplice, let's call her Jenny, has been alerted to the face that it is her turn to perform, because this is the only trick you do which starts by you taking any nine cards from the pack. So she is waiting for you to say 'Now who's going to help me with this trick?' She is very quick to reply 'I will' before anybody else can stake a claim. You say 'Thank you Jenny. I'm afraid this trick involves you leaving the room while we choose a card, but it will only be for a minute or two.'

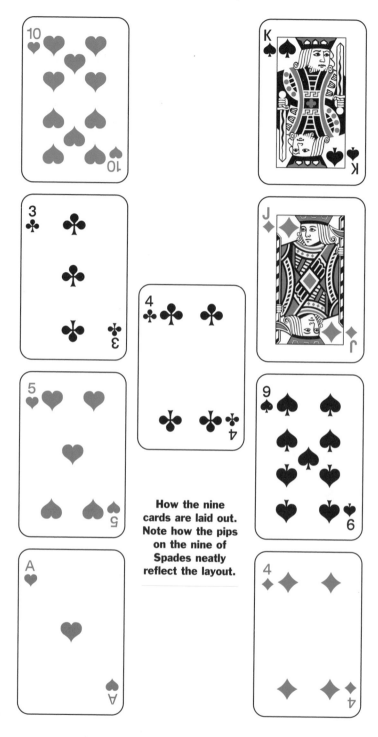

How the nine cards are laid out. Note how the pips on the nine of Spades neatly reflect the layout.

4 As Jenny leaves the room, you pick up the nine cards and deal them face up as above. Notice that the cards are laid out as if they were the spots on the nine. When finished, ask someone in the audience to point to any of the nine cards. Jenny is now called back. You tell her that she must identify the card selected by the audience. Tell her that you will point to the cards in turn and that when you point to the chosen card she must stop you.

5 Begin pointing to the cards at random with a pencil, saying 'Is it this one?' or 'This one?' or 'What about this?' As soon as you point to the chosen card, Jenny will say: 'Yes, that's the one.'

6 It is vital for you to remember to point to the nine before you point to the chosen card. When you point to the nine your pencil touches the spot on the nine which corresponds to the chosen card. Jenny immediately knows which is the card she has to identify. For example, in the illustration suppose the chosen card was the five of Hearts. You might start by pointing to the Jack of Diamonds, then three of Clubs, then nine of Spades (taking care that the tip of the pencil touches the pip on the card one from the bottom in the left-hand row). Jenny knows now that the chosen card is the five of Hearts, and as soon as you point to that, she says so.

8 If the chosen card is by chance the nine itself, it doesn't matter. When you point to it you merely point to the

AFTERTHOUGHT

What happens if when you lay out the nine cards from the top of the pack there happens to be two (or even three) nines in the layout? Excellent! It improves the trick. All Jenny has to know is that in the case of two nines, the important one is the first one you point to. When you repeat the trick you could use the other nine as the master card. That should make it even harder for somebody to spot how you do it.

spot corresponding to the nine, in the example illustrated, the next to bottom spot in the right hand row.

9 You can repeat this trick, while the audience slowly works out how you do it. Some will realise immediately that Jenny must be an accomplice. I like to throw them off the scent by making the chosen card the fifth one both times. If somebody says 'I know how it's done,' send Jenny from the room and let that person try it. If they succeed, you'll know if it were a fluke or not. If they really have spotted the trick, congratulate them, ask them to keep it a secret and move onto the next trick. If they fail, ask an onlooker to shuffle the nine cards and lay them out again. It makes no difference. Repeat the trick a third time and then say that that's it for today.

Odds and ends

Mind reading

● ●

Skill level 2

You will need
Any ten cards and an accomplice.

The trick
Any ten cards are dealt out on the table. With the magician's back turned, a spectator is asked to touch one so that all those present, except the magician, can see which card he touches. The magician then turns and examines the cards closely. By asking the spectator to concentrate on first colour, then rank, of the chosen card, the magician can name it.

● ●

How to do it
This trick is given a skill factor of 2, although no special skills are required. Its effect depends upon the level of deception by which the accomplice conveys to you the identity of the card, and the natural way in which you can receive the information without revealing what is going on.

1 The ten cards are laid out to correspond to the pips on a 10 (see opposite). Your accomplice, as in the trick called 'One over the Eight' is Jenny (since one accomplice is enough for any magician). Jenny, of course, knows the card that the spectator (let's call him Lee) has touched.

2 When you turn round, examine the cards closely, frowning in concentration if you like. Look up as if you are puzzled and glance round your audience. Pass quickly over Jenny. She is in fact, signalling the card in question through the position of her hands.

3 For the card at the top of the left-hand column (the three of Spades in the illustration), she has her right hand on her left shoulder. For the next card down (four of Diamonds) her hand is between shoulder and elbow. For the next card down (Ace of Clubs) it rests on her left forearm. For the bottom card in the left-hand column (five of Hearts) her right hand is covering her left.

4 For any card in the right-hand column, Jenny signals in the same way, except that her left hand is resting in position on her right arm. This leaves the two cards in the centre column. For the top one (i.e. farthest from you as you look at the layout) her hand is touching her chin, neck or lips, for the bottom one her hands are straight down by her sides.

5 Once you have received the message from Jenny, scratch your head. This tells her she can give up her pose and relax.

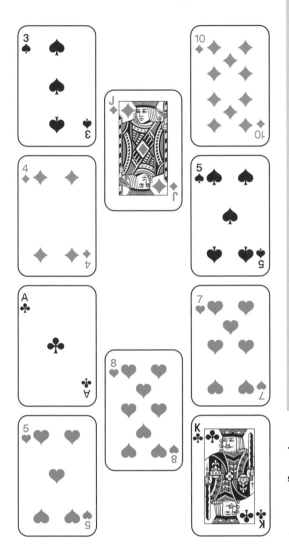

NOTE

This is a trick you can perform two or three times, with different volunteers from the audience. There is nothing to prevent Jenny herself being one of them. She should choose the lower centre card, since leaving her arms straight by her sides is probably the most natural pose, and everybody else will be looking at her, as well as you. It is more interesting, I think, if you deal out a fresh set of ten cards each time you do the trick.

The layout for Mind reading. The signals to represent each of the cards are discussed in the text.

6 You now have to extract suspense from revealing the card. Do not just blurt it out. Ask Lee to concentrate on the card's colour. Let's say the card he chose is the seven of Hearts (Jenny's left hand was clutching her right forearm). Say 'I feel a touch of red. I'm pretty sure it's a red card. Just concentrate on its rank now Lee.' By chance, the layout contains the eight and five of Hearts as well as the seven, so say 'This is very difficult because it could either be the seven or eight of Hearts. I think it's higher than five. In fact, my opinion is that the card you are thinking of, Lee, is the seven of Hearts.'

Hypnosis

Skill level 2

You will need
Any 12 cards and an accomplice.

The trick
A spectator leaves the room. The 12 cards from the top of a shuffled pack are then laid out in three rows of four cards. A member of the audience selects one of the 12 cards. The person who left the room is asked to return. The magician touches the cards one by one in haphazard fashion, saying 'Is it this one? This? What about this?' and the spectator replies: 'I don't think so, No' until eventually the chosen card is touched, and the answer is 'Yes'.

How to do it
The person who leaves the room is your accomplice, Jenny. You prepare her to be ready for this trick by means of any phrase which you pre-arrange with her, such as 'I'm now about to do an experiment involving a form of hypnotism, of which like all practitioners of the cult of magic, I am a master.'

1 You are holding the pack of cards as you say this, and you have already noted the bottom card of the pack. Let us say it is the six of Hearts. While you speak you hold the pack face up in such a way that everybody, and in particular Jenny, can see that the bottom card is the six of Hearts. This is the key card, which both of you know and remember.

2 The audience, of course, will not notice, since they do not know what is to happen. You then say 'Now many people are frightened of any suggestion of hypnotism – I think they fear they are going to be put under the spell and never recover. I am not going to go this far. I am merely going to impose my will upon the subject so that he or she will pick up my vibes and choose a card which I indicate. Now can I have a volunteer?'

3 Jenny will call 'Me,' and put her hand up immediately, so that you can say 'I think Jenny was the first to put her hand up, so let's try to put the influence on her. First of all, Jenny, would you mind, please, leaving the room?'

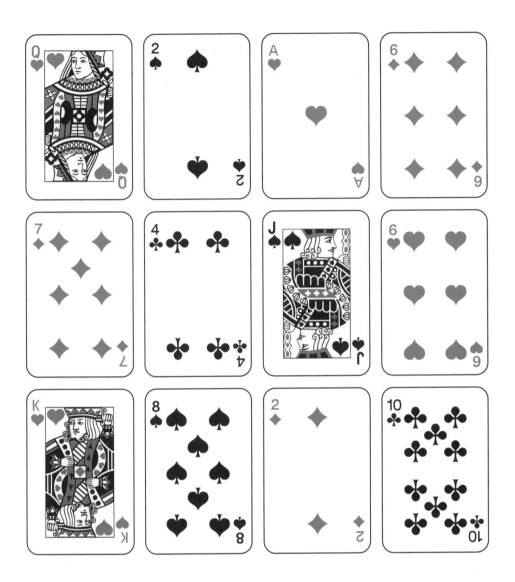

The layout for Hypnosis.

4 Once Jenny has gone, say 'Right – now to show there's no collusion or anything, I will shuffle the cards.' You then execute a normal shuffle, but make sure that the last set of cards you transfer from your right hand to your left consists of only four of five cards. This will ensure that the bottom card (six of Hearts) is the fourth or fifth from the top of the pack. You can, if you are confident enough, now repeat the shuffle twice, transferring the top half-dozen cards back to the bottom and then back again to the top. The only object is to make sure that the six of hearts ends among the top 12.

5 You now deal the top 12 cards to the layout (see above) and ask one audience member to pick one of them. When everybody knows the chosen card,

● ● ● ● ● ● ● ● ● ● ● ● ● ● ● ● ●

you tell the audience that when Jenny returns you are going to point to the cards in no particular order, asking Jenny in turn if this is the chosen card. Explain that she will say 'No,' to each until you point to the correct card, when you are going to convey a strong hypnotic message to her which will impel her to say: 'Yes.' You then ask Jenny to return.

6 You explain to Jenny that a particular card from among the 12 on the table has been selected by the audience. You go on to say 'I am going to point to the cards one by one in no particular order, but when I point to the chosen card you should feel an inner voice telling you to say "Yes". This will be my mind communicating with yours in a manner similar to hypnosis. You must obey your impulse and say: "Yes". You will know when the time comes. Is this clear?' Jenny will agree that it is clear.

7 All you do now is point to cards at random. Sooner or later you will point to the key card, the six of Hearts, asking: 'Is it this one?' Jenny will pause fractionally and say 'I don't think so.' You will then point to two other cards, to which Jenny will say 'No', but when you point to the third one after the key card Jenny will say 'Yes.' You tell her she's picked the right card. if she's a good

NOTE

Do you know why it is suggested that Jenny says 'I don't think so,' or 'I'm not sure, I think not,' when you point to the key card? The answer is that it is possible (it should happen about once in 12 times) that the audience's chosen card is the six of Hearts. In this case, when you first point to this card and Jenny says 'I don't think so,' you can pass on to two more cards and then return to the six of Hearts again. Jenny can now say 'Yes,' and add 'You know I had this faint feeling it was that one the first time you pointed to it, but this time I'm absolutely certain.'

If you are performing this trick more than once, you should in your pointing routine, point to one or two cards twice. This conditions the audience to think nothing of it when you're forced to do it by reason of their choosing the key card.

actress she can go further and say 'It's strange, I had this compulsion come over me to say "Yes." I can't explain it, but I just knew somehow that that was the one.'

Index

Acknowledgments

Executive Editor Trevor Davies
Editor Rachel Lawrence
Design Manager Tokiko Morishima
Designer Les Needham
Illustrations
Line + Line and Publish on Demand Ltd
Production Controller Jo Sim

BUENOS DÍAS